Catholic Women Preach

Catholic Women Preach

Raising Voices, Renewing the Church

CYCLE C

Elizabeth Donnelly and Russ Petrus, Editors

ORBIS BOOKS
Maryknoll, New York 10545

Founded in 1970, Orbis Books endeavors to publish works that enlighten the mind, nourish the spirit, and challenge the conscience. The publishing arm of the Maryknoll Fathers and Brothers, Orbis seeks to explore the global dimensions of the Christian faith and mission, to invite dialogue with diverse cultures and religious traditions, and to serve the cause of reconciliation and peace. The books published reflect the views of their authors and do not represent the official position of the Maryknoll Society. To learn more about Maryknoll and Orbis Books, please visit our website at www.orbisbooks.com.

Library of Congress Cataloging-in-Publication Data

Names: Donnelly, Elizabeth A., editor. | Petrus, Russ, editor.
Title: Catholic women preach : raising voices, renewing the church—Cycle C / Elizabeth Donnelly and Russ Petrus, editors.
Description: Maryknoll, NY : Orbis Books, [2024] | Summary: "Homilies by an international cast of Catholic women follow the liturgical readings for Cycle C"— Provided by publisher.
Identifiers: LCCN 2024008800 (print) | LCCN 2024008801 (ebook) | ISBN 9781626985810 (trade paperback) | ISBN 9798888660362 (epub)
Classification: LCC BX1756.A2 C39 2024 (print) | LCC BX1756.A2 (ebook) | DDC 252/.02—dc23/eng/20240326
LC record available at https://lccn.loc.gov/2024008800
LC ebook record available at https://lccn.loc.gov/2024008801

Contents

CHRISTMAS SEASON

LENT

EASTER SEASON

CONTENTS

ORDINARY TIME*

Editor's note: Homilies in this volume were given during Cycle B in previous years, when in some cases (here the ninth through twelfth Sundays in Ordinary Time) solemnities took precedence.

CONTENTS

CONTENTS

Foreword

Mary Catherine Hilkert, OP

In his first apostolic exhortation, *Evangelii Gaudium (The Joy of the Gospel)*, Pope Francis challenged the Church to accept what he described as "this unruly freedom of the word, which accomplishes what it wills in ways that surpass our calculations and ways of thinking."* His call to all the baptized to realize our identity as missionary disciples echoes the message of Pope Paul VI in 1975, ten years after the closing of the Second Vatican Council, in his apostolic exhortation *Evangelii Nuntiandi (Evangelization Today)*. Both exhortations were addressed to all the baptized, and both emphasize that the Holy Spirit is the source and cause of all effective proclamation and hearing of the Gospel.† Each speaks with confidence of the power of the Spirit to transform both Church and world in and through the proclamation of the Word of God and urges contemporary believers to take up that challenge. Two burning questions that Pope Paul raised in 1975 continue to confront the Church today:

---

*Pope Francis, *Evangelii Gaudium (The Joy of the Gospel)*, 22.

†*Evangelii Nuntiandi (Evangelization Today)*, 75; *Evangelii Gaudium*, 119–20 and *passim*.

In our day, what has happened to that hidden energy of the Good News, which is able to have a powerful effect on the conscience of human persons?

To what extent and in what way is that evangelical force capable of really transforming the people of this century?*

Both apostolic exhortations turn to the event of Pentecost to celebrate what is possible for disciples gathered together in prayer in and through the power of the Spirit. In a similar vein, the Synod on Synodality, like the Second Vatican Council, has been referred to as a "new Pentecost" evoking the event during which the Spirit first formed the Church. From the first phase of listening sessions, which took place in contemporary "upper rooms" and church basements around the world, two of the concerns that echoed repeatedly were the calls for more effective preaching and for recognition of women's baptismal dignity, including full and equal participation in the life and decision-making of the Church.

The Working Document for the Continental Stage (DCS) of the synodal process, "Enlarge the Space of your Tent (Isaiah 54:2)," stated that the quality of homilies was reported as a problem "almost universally." A major part of the problem, according to the report on the global listening sessions, was

the distance between the content of the sermon, the beauty of faith and the concreteness of life; and the separation between the liturgical life of the assembly and the family network of the community.... [Participants called for] "deeper homilies, centered on the

---

Evangelii Nuntiandi, 4.

Gospel and the readings of the day, and not on politics, making use of accessible and attractive language that refers to the life of the faithful."*

This volume, *Catholic Women Preach: Raising Voices, Renewing the Church, Cycle C*—like the previous two volumes for Liturgical Cycles A and B—offers abundant witness to the fact that the Spirit of God continues to raise up surprising and gifted preachers whose faithful witness and prophetic speech offer the entire Church both challenge and hope.

Pope Francis's naming of the "unruly freedom of the word" and "infinite creativity of the Spirit," evident throughout the preachings in this volume, has clear roots in the Pentecost narrative depicted in the opening chapters of the Acts of the Apostles.† In Christian art, and in the imagination of many, that scene is often visualized as tongues of fire descending on Mary and eleven male disciples. At the annual liturgical celebrations of the feast of Pentecost, the reading from the second chapter of the Acts is frequently proclaimed in multiple languages to remind the worshiping assembly that the crowd gathered at that first Pentecost were from diverse regions and spoke many different languages.

That text speaks of the initial amazement and confusion of the gathered crowd who heard the Good News proclaimed in their own language. What is often overlooked, however, is the earlier reference in the first chapter of Acts to those who were gathered in that upper room—not only the eleven male apostles, but, also "*[t]here were some women in their company, and Mary, the mother of Jesus and his brothers*" (Acts 1:14).

---

*"*Enlarge the space of your tent* (Isaiah 54:2)," Working Document for the Continental Stage (DCS): For a Synodal Church, 2021–2024, Vatican City: General Secretariat for the Synod, October 2022, 93.

†See Pope Francis, *Evangelii Gaudium* #22, 178.

Likewise, when the descent of the Holy Spirit is described in chapter 2, the text says, "*All* were filled with the Holy Spirit. They began to express themselves in foreign tongues and make bold proclamations as the Spirit prompted them" (italics added). When Peter preaches about what they all have experienced, he describes this Pentecost event as an experience of prophetic utterance and compares it to the promise of the prophet Joel that in the future God's own Spirit would be poured out lavishly on God's beloved people:

> Your sons and daughters shall prophesy,
> the young shall see visions
> and the old shall dream dreams.
> Yes, even on my servants and handmaids
> I will pour out a portion of my spirit in those days,
> and they shall prophesy. (Acts 2:16–18)

The good news of the inbreaking of the reign of God includes not only the message proclaimed but also the surprise of those who are chosen as messengers to announce the mystery of God and God's ways. The Spirit's prophetic gifts are distributed widely to daughters and sons, young and old, servants and handmaids. Those gifts include charisms for prophecy and exhortation. The current Synod on Synodality includes a clear focus on the baptismal dignity, vocation, and mission of all of the baptized. With a similar concern in a speech at the Second Vatican Council, Cardinal Suenens challenged his brother bishops to consider their pastoral experience:

> Does not each one of us know lay people, both men and women, in his own diocese who are truly called by God? These people have received various different charisms from the Spirit, for catechesis, evangelization, apostolic action of various types. . . . Without

these charisms, the ministry of the Church would be impoverished and sterile.*

As we approach the sixtieth anniversary of the closing of the Second Vatican Council, the fiftieth anniversary of *Evangelii Nuntiandi,* and the second session of the Synod on Synodality in October 2024, the words of Pope Paul VI in 1975 ring more true than ever: People listen more willingly to witnesses than to teachers, and if they listen to teachers, it is because they are witnesses.† The witness of faithful women who can testify from experience that they have found in the Gospel "words of spirit and life" (John 6:63) is essential to the mission of the entire Church. May the bold proclamations of the Gospel in this volume prompt a wider hearing of the Good News and lead contemporary disciples to "hear the word of God and act on it" (Luke 11:28).

---

*As quoted by Albert Vanhoye, SJ, "The Biblical Question of Charisms After Vatican II," in *Vatican II: Assessment and Perspectives Twenty-Five Years After* (1962–87), ed. Rene Latourelle (New York: Paulist Press, 1988), 439–68 at 442–43.

†*Evangelii Nuntiandi,* 41.

Introduction

Elizabeth Donnelly and Russ Petrus

We are delighted to offer this third volume of innovative and nourishing homilies from the Catholic Women Preach website, this time for Lectionary Cycle C. (Orbis Books published the Cycle A volume in 2022 and Cycle B in 2023.) As in the previous volumes, we were blessed to be able to choose from two cycles of homilies, in this case from 2018–19 and 2021–22. Again, it was a challenge to select which preaching to include in the printed volume, but all homilies—now nearly 475!—remain fully accessible on the website. Simply type in a scripture reference, key word(s), or preacher name in the search box to access exceptional preaching by diverse Catholic women from around the world.

We go to print anticipating the second session at the Vatican of the Synod on Synodality, a multiyear journey inviting all of us to listen deeply to one another and imagine a more welcoming and mission-driven Catholic community. We were delighted and encouraged that the participants in the October 2023 meeting in their final synthesis report prioritized the need for women's greater co-responsible leadership in the Church, ongoing consideration of restoring women to the diaconate, and greater opportunities for lay preaching at the Eucharist.

As we go to print, the Catholic Women Preach website has been visited nearly two million times, and our videos have been viewed 560,000 times, engaging viewers in 45,000 hours or nearly 2.7 million minutes of experiencing Catholic women preach. It is clear that the project both highlights and helps to satisfy the longing for the voices and contributions of women in our Church.

Once again, we are deeply grateful to the members of the Catholic Women Preach founding committee. In addition to us, they include Jocelyn Collen, Sr. Diana Culbertson, Rita Houlihan, and Deborah Rose. Betty Anne is forever grateful that she discovered that the FutureChurch team had a similar vision of lifting up women's voices. Many hours of dedicated collaboration and planning led us to launch the website with preaching for Advent in 2016.

We would also like to thank those who offered editorial assistance in the first years of the website: Diana Culbertson, OP; Marianne Race, CSJ; Janet Schlichting, OP; and Mary Ann Wiesemann-Mills, OP.

We also are most grateful for the wise counsel and support of our distinguished advisory board members: M. Shawn Copeland; Richard Gaillardetz (deceased); Thomas Groome; Nontando Hadebe; Mary Catherine Hilkert, OP; James Keenan, SJ; Raymond Kemp; Paul Lakeland; Astrid Lobo Gajiwala; James Martin, SJ; Rhonda Miska; Carolyn Osiek, RSCJ; Brian Pierce, OP; Christine Schenk, CSJ; and Jude Siciliano, OP. We mourn Rick's passing and are consoled by the assurance that his rich legacy of teaching and writing on what makes for a vibrant Church community will continue to animate future generations.

Once again we warmly thank Robert Ellsberg for encouraging us to edit this three-volume collection for the lectionary cycle. He and the entire Orbis team have consistently been superb, responsive, and mission driven.

Our heartfelt thanks go again to Kelly Sankowski for her stellar editorial assistance. Kelly communicated with each of the sixty-two contributors we selected, proposed titles for the reflections, and compiled all the edits and changes to the texts and updates to the bios. It was a monumental task, which Kelly made look easy.

We are also most grateful to our friend and advisor Cathy Hilkert, OP, for her remarkable foreword. She has taught and written more about preaching and women's voices in preaching than perhaps anyone, and her wisdom and insight are a true gift to the entire Church.

Once again, we are delighted to feature the gorgeous work of Laura James, this time, *Woman Preaching* (acrylic on canvas, 2008), on the cover. Please visit her inspiring website, www.laurajamesart.com.

We especially thank and commend the sixty-two contributors themselves. Catholic Women Preach would not exist without the extraordinary, faith-filled, insightful women whose wisdom and witness have helped us make sense of our lived realities and more tenaciously follow the path of discipleship in today's world. We hope that over the course of the liturgical year you will be nourished and challenged by these companions on the road.

Finally, we are honored to have been able to include preaching for the Twenty-eighth Sunday in Ordinary Time from Shawnee M. Daniels-Sykes, PhD, both on the website and in these pages. Dr. Daniel-Sykes passed away on October 31, 2022, at the age of sixty-one. A trail-blazing and pioneering Black Catholic ethicist, she is sorely missed, but her contributions continue to gift us all and call us to better ourselves, our world, and our Church.

ADVENT

First Sunday of Advent

What seeds will we sow this Advent?

CARMEN SAMMUT, MSOLA

Jeremiah 33:14–16
Psalm 25:4–5, 8–9, 10, 14
1 Thessalonians 3:12—4:2
Luke 21:25–28, 34–36

Today we enter the Advent Season, a time of waiting in joyful hope for the coming of Our Savior Jesus Christ. It is a time when we prepare to commemorate Jesus's coming in Bethlehem, as one of us, two thousand years ago; a time to be aware and live fully from his constant presence with us each day, and to wait for his second coming.

When I was a child in Malta, on this first Sunday of Advent my mother would gather us children together and have us sow some seeds, which we would plant in the dark earth. Every Sunday we would water them, and look at how they were growing, and compare them to see whose had grown the most. And we would look forward to using them at Christmas to decorate the crib.

Today I see this custom as symbolic of what we are called to during this season. What are the seeds we want to sow at the beginning of this Advent season? The first reading suggests the seeds of justice, peace, and security and reminds us that God fulfills the promise made to us, that these seeds will grow and bear fruit. Yet, as we are reminded in the Gospel, our experience is often one of disasters beyond our control, not to mention those which are caused by our own recklessness and sin. What we sow is also what we reap. We see the consequences of our ways of living in what is happening to our planet, and of our ways of relating with one another in daily news items about exclusion, human trafficking, the pain of victims of sexual abuse and violence, the migration of whole populations. . . . .

However, the readings for this Sunday tell us that the seeds of redemption will grow and bear fruit. The promise will be fulfilled, not by some sort of magic, but through us who wait in joyful hope and in constant prayer for the coming of Our Savior Jesus Christ. Nations will be in dismay and perplexed, and some people will die of fright, yet those who still hope can stand erect and raise their heads, because they read the signs as an opportunity for a decision to love others and to receive the gift of redemption.

Dismay, perplexity, and fear can paralyze us. They can stop us from taking the needed action at the appropriate moment. Standing up enables us to see and show up when and where we are needed. The plants grow in the dark, where it may be difficult to see positive strength at work. We are called to recognize Jesus, the Emmanuel, God-with-us, God never without us, not in the spectacular but in every person we meet, especially those we would normally exclude and in the small details and gestures we often fail to notice. Our societies and our politicians often try to make us afraid of each other, so as to stop us from welcoming the stranger, the migrant, the one who needs our help. Yet being able to stand up helps us go against the flow. It allows us to make the decision to go out of ourselves and our own preoccupations and truly love and care for one another and for our planet. Indeed, in so doing, we are welcoming Jesus, the one who came and will come again, the one who is present among us.

I came to understand something of what this could call us to in 2011 when I was living in Tunis during the revolution there. The crowds were all singing their national anthem, which includes the words: "We will die but our nation will live." They were ready to give up their lives so that their children could inherit a better life. They could stand up when everything around them was crumbling.

We, too, are called to give our lives so that others may live. So much has crumbled in the Church and in societies all over the world. This is producing injustice, unrest, strife for countless numbers of people. As we recognize this, we ask that the Lord may "make us increase and abound in love for one another and for all people." May our love be the gift of our lives, and may we hasten the coming of our Lord Jesus Christ for everyone we meet. May we thus be bearers of hope, sowers of hope wherever we are.

May our plants be most beautiful as we place them next to the crib this Christmas. May our most precious seeds bear fruit in our ability to recognize the coming of Jesus in every person we meet. May this season of Advent be filled with blessings for all God's children.

Second Sunday of Advent
We'll never be the same

MARY ELLEN GREEN, OP

Baruch 5:1–9
Psalm 126:1–2, 2–3, 4–5, 6
Philippians 1:4–6, 8–11
Luke 3:1–6

The author of Luke's Gospel must have been a born journalist. He/she begins the narrative by anticipating and answering all the important questions: When? Where? What? Who? How? Why? It's all there as we are introduced to this singular moment in history, this pivotal event in the story of the human race and their God, this dramatic announcement of an exciting, transforming opportunity for all who are listening. This is the first and official proclamation of the gospel by John the Baptizer.

Imagine yourself there in the crowd, waiting in curious attention, scintillating anticipation, and tingling expectancy to hear what this strange man has to say. How do you feel as you listen to this new message? Excited? Nervous? Skeptical? Hopeful?

Look around you to see who's with you. What is their reaction?

Take a moment to define with the same historical exactitude this time in our own lives. Who is it that rules the world we live in? The state? The city? The community? The Church? What is the context of our own story as we listen with itching ears? Who are we and where are we as we enter into this Advent invitation?

The reality of the global pandemic lingers with us. We know the suffering, challenges, and upheaval we have all experienced over the last months. How have we changed? How are we there for one another?

Touch into the longing in your mind and heart for an answer to our search for peace and justice, for kindness and compassion. Who is speaking to us and how? Who are the prophets of our world calling out to us from the wilderness of our existence where we wait to hear that word of hope? Will God's kingdom ever come? Will God's will ever be done on earth as it is in heaven?

It's all about repentance, isn't it? METANOIA! The Greek word METANOIA includes much more than just examining our conscience and going to confession. METANOIA means a change of mind and heart, a complete turning around at the deepest level, the kind of inner transformation that bears visible fruit. This time it's for real. This time it's serious. Our Savior is coming and we have to be prepared.

I think of so many of our religious congregations, my own included, that are going through seismic changes at this time. Buildings are being taken down or repurposed or sold. The land that we have come to love is being developed by someone else. Our members are getting old and dying. There are few if any new members.

What does this mean for our own conversion process, personally and collectively? To what new place are we being called? What's on the horizon for our future? What will be our new identity, our new mission as we evolve?

What are the mountains in our personal and communal lives that have to be brought down and leveled? What are the valleys that have to be raised? What are the crooked ways that have to be straightened? It's construction time, folks, and we have to get going. Something's happening. Someone's coming into our lives and we'll never be the same.

Pope Francis calls us in *Laudato Sí* to what he calls "ecological conversion." How is our spiritual conversion linked to our relationship with our dear Mother Earth?

In our first reading from Baruch, the prophet, we hear more excitement, more anticipation as he reminds us that the time has, indeed, come: "Up, Jerusalem! Stand upon the heights; look to the east and the west at the word of the Holy One, rejoicing that they are remembered by God."

I don't know about you, but Advent always stirs me up spiritually. There's something about the gladness of the season, the joy in the air, and the elation in the atmosphere that makes me happy and hopeful. I want to believe and I do believe that Jesus is the reason for the season.

How about you?

Third Sunday of Advent

Mastering the rejoice choice

ELYSE GALLOWAY

Zephaniah 3:14–18a
Isaiah 12:2–3, 4, 5–6
Philippians 4:4–7
Luke 3:10–18

Gaudete—Latin for "rejoice." The readings today focus on re-joicing in the Lord and our tradition of Christian joy. We're told to be glad and exult with our whole hearts. The responsorial psalm tells us to be confident and unafraid. Paul instructs us to rejoice at all times.

But let's be real. It's hard. It's hard to be happy all the time. To not let anxiety cripple our inner sense of peace. Or have doubt creep into those vulnerable moments and have us question God's presence.

Just two weeks ago, in the midst of preparing this sermon, I found myself doing just that—questioning where God was in the middle of my difficulties. Downhearted, uncertain, and fearful of the future. Beyond my own personal situations, I grew increasingly upset looking at the state of the world, with global trends of discrimination, poverty, violence, and so much more.

I wanted to sit down with Paul and tell him all the reasons why his charge to rejoice continuously was unrealistic. Tell him that, looking at all the circumstances of the world, there are so many reasons we have for living without joy.

I even questioned how Paul could have lived a life of joy. Beatings, shipwrecks, imprisonment, danger everywhere he went, and likely feeling the pressure of being spiritually responsible for all the new churches.

How could someone who experienced so much adversity teach us to rejoice always?

Well, I think it's because Paul understood that happiness is ultimately a choice. It's a choice that is built on an awareness and acceptance of God's presence and power operating in our lives.

If we look at the readings for today, we are inundated with reminders of God's presence. The King of Israel, the LORD is in your midst. The LORD is at hand. For among you is the great and Holy One of Israel.

He is in every moment and every situation.

Not only that, but we as Christians have a sacred right to happiness. Acknowledging the proper source of this happiness is the most important thing and the key to accessing it.

I, like many, sometimes made the mistake of believing that happiness was tied to my circumstances—who I was with, what I was doing, where I was in my life. My circumstances determined my level of happiness.

But with God, happiness has absolutely nothing to do with circumstances. Circumstances are temporary, while our relationship and life with God is eternal. We are to lean into this perspective, choosing to make it part of our being.

And our dear friend Paul did just that. Despite the difficulties he faced, Paul was still happy. Why? Because he focused his thoughts and feelings on God's promise of an abundant life. In rooting his sense of himself and his well-being in his eternal and invaluable relationship with God, he was able to live in such a way that no worldly circumstances could ever affect the internal joy he experienced by living each day with God. In opting to make this perspective part of his being, Paul made what I call the "rejoice choice"—choosing to rejoice always and in all circumstances. And with that came happiness and what Paul describes as a peace that surpasses all understanding.

What could be better than that?

But like all great things, making the choice to rejoice requires intention. It requires a conscious decision to do so each day, making use of practices to shift and develop a new perspective that will become part of who we are. Whether it's speaking daily affirmations into our life, engaging in mindfulness, or cultivating an attitude of thankfulness and gratitude, we need to find practices that tie our happiness to a divine relationship with God.

This Gaudete Sunday and all days going forward, I challenge myself and all of you to master the rejoice choice. Choose to rejoice—because God provides us with too many reasons to be counted.

Fourth Sunday of Advent

How will we labor with God?

SARA FAIRBANKS, OP

Micah 5:1–4a
Palm 80:2–3, 15–16, 18–19
Hebrews 10:5–10
Luke 1:39–45

Two lowly women of Judea, living under the subjugation of the Roman Empire, meet under the most extraordinary circumstances to share the great things God has done for them. The elderly, childless Elizabeth has now conceived a son. The teenage Mary has been visited by an angel and through the power of the Holy Spirit will bear the Messiah, God's Son, whose reign will have no end. Sharing their stories of faith, they are lifted up in God's grace. They know in a new way their value and dignity in the eyes of God. Elizabeth, filled with the Holy Spirit, says to Mary, "Blest are you among women, and blest is the fruit of your womb" (Lk 1:42).

And Mary says, "My soul magnifies my God, and my spirit rejoices in God my Savior, for the Holy One has looked with favor on me a lowly servant" (Lk 1:46–48).

On these mystical heights, Mary prophesies about God's coming reign of justice and peace: "The powerful will be brought down from their thrones, and the lowly lifted up!

The hungry will be filled with good things, and the rich sent away empty" (Lk 1:46–53). Mary's visit to Elizabeth strengthens the bonds of sisterhood between them for the challenges ahead. And both will suffer.

Like Elizabeth and Mary, Christians through the ages have known that God's grace is both gift and responsibility. The Dominican mystic Meister Eckhart once remarked, "What is the good to me of Mary's being full of grace if I am not full also? What does it profit me the Father's giving his Son birth unless I bear him too?"

The season of Advent reminds us that this ancient biblical story, with its abundant grace and its costly responsibility, must become our story.

This story of Elizabeth and Mary birthing God's Word and laboring for God's reign on earth was enfleshed in a new way by the African men and women enslaved in colonial America. During the first hundred years of slavery in the United States, some Catholics and a few Protestant denominations began slowly and sparingly to teach their African slaves the Christian faith, highlighting, of course, that they should serve their slave masters as they would serve Christ. Most slaveowners at this time, however, prohibited their slaves from Christian worship or instruction because they "were not willing to raise slaves above the level of animal property and thus concede that they were buying and selling souls worthy of saving."*

Nevertheless, as slave narratives tell us, Black preachers began to emerge, and small groups of slaves would sneak into the woods to pray and sing together. In their lowliness, God visited them. They, too, were filled with grace and experienced a freeing of their spirits. Lifted high in God's love, they

---

*Henry H. Mitchell, *Black Preaching: The Recovery of a Powerful Art* (Nashville, TN: Abingdon Press, 1991), 24.

felt their value and dignity as human beings made in God's image. Like Elizabeth and Mary, they trusted that nothing was impossible for God, who they believed would deliver their descendants from slavery.

A Black preacher in North Carolina named Isaac freely embraced the costly discipleship needed to bring about God's reign on earth. One night he held a secret prayer meeting in the woods and was caught by the slave master. Isaac was flogged for preaching the Gospel. His master then poured salty brine on his back. When Isaac was nearly well, he was flogged again, and this went on and on until he died.*

When I first heard this story, I felt pride and admiration for our African brothers and sisters who resisted the cruel oppression and religious persecution perpetrated by our nation. I also felt shame and guilt to see the hateful bigotry and selfish inhumanity of our country. Like the Roman Empire, our country has subjugated other peoples for its own profit and prosperity. Pax Romana looks a lot like Pax Americana. A culture of racism continues in our own day. White privilege goes on promoting unfair social and economic benefits for white citizens while subjecting people of color to cruel discrimination and costly disadvantages.

As we celebrate the birth of Christ this Christmas, how can we birth Christ in our time and culture? What steps can we take to overcome racial injustices in our country? Like Elizabeth and Mary, will we, too, be full of grace? How will we labor with God, who brings down the powerful and lifts up the lowly, so that as sisters and brothers we may live in dignity and equality as the one family of God?

---

*Mitchell, *Black Preaching*, 29.

CHRISTMAS SEASON

Christmas

Trusting in God's constancy

Yadira Vieyra Alvarez

Isaiah 9:1–6
Psalm 96:1–2, 2–3, 11–12, 13
Titus 2:11–14
Luke 2:1–14

Today's readings remind me of how the joy of Christmas is present even in difficult circumstances.

A few years ago, as my family gathered to celebrate our Christmas Eve dinner, my mother received notice that my aunt had attempted to cross the United States border, hoping to be reunited with her young children. Her attempt was unsuccessful and she had been detained. Even though the message was clear, it seemed my mother was in denial. She asked me to explain the text message to her. As I did so, my mom's eyes filled with tears.

That Christmas was full of uncertainty and pain for my mother, but it was also a day of prayer for us—a day of gratitude for the birth of Jesus Christ. God has provided for my family all these years. He has always been with us, and his constancy in our lives has been overwhelming. That Christmas, we had to trust in him and let the news of the birth of

17

our Savior bring us out of a dark place to experience a renewed sense of hope.

In our reading from the Book of Isaiah, we begin with the imagery of the Israelites walking in darkness and then seeing a great light. This light brings about a new kind of joy: one that arrives through the birth of a son. But it isn't just any child being born—it's the Son of God. We hear that this son will have a vastly different type of dominion from the ones people have experienced, dominions marked by turmoil and uncertainty; his dominion will be "forever peaceful." This same light—this same peace-bearing child—is the one born into our lives. We must remember, however, that receiving this child is a decision. If we do not accept and embrace the presence of Jesus in our daily lives, of what use is his peaceful dominion? If we do not have peace in our families, our homes, our marriages, of what use is God's offering to us?

That same challenge is present alongside the joy that is found in our psalm: "They shall exult before the Lord, for he comes; for he comes to rule the earth. He shall rule the world with justice and the peoples with his constancy." Christ is born to bring constancy—meaning faithfulness—commitment, dedication. The challenge lies in having the eyes to see it. We despair often, and our own selfishness, pride, and worries blind us to God's presence. Constancy is necessary for our souls, but do we believe that God has been constantly with us? Do we accept his faithfulness? His faithfulness is not the problem; our recognition of it and our lack of reciprocity is. God is here. He has always been here. Today's psalm calls each one of us to open our eyes.

Christmas gives us a new opportunity to trust in his loyalty to us. Mary is the epitome of this mutual commitment. Mary, a young woman, found favor in God's eyes. God chose her to be the bearer of Jesus's humanity. Mary rejoiced. Mary trusted. She was selected to not just carry the Son of God in her womb but to live through the full experience of birth in the most impoverished circumstances. Not in a private maternity suite, followed by a recovery suite with state-of-the-art labor and delivery equipment. Not in a hospital lockdown unit, a place where Mary and Joseph and their baby could be safe and even have some privacy. The Son of God was born in a manger surrounded by animals and was wrapped only in swaddling clothes. Yet Mary continued to trust, and even to rejoice.

In the Gospel of John, Jesus said to his disciples, "When a woman is in labor, she has pain, because her hour has come, but when her child is born, her anguish turns into joy because she has brought a human being into the world." Mary is filled with a deep sense of joy. The reason for the joy is the birth of Jesus Christ, the only Son of God, and so for us too, the reason we can experience joy is because of the birth of God's Son. Mary and Joseph needed no lavish accommodations to fully appreciate the joy of hope that came with the birth of Jesus Christ. Pope Francis talks about Christian joy as something that cannot be bought, something that is a gift from God. It is a pure joy, the kind of joy that marked the birth of Jesus.

The God of the universe was really born; he walked among us and opened the doors to eternal life.

Even more wonderful, he walks with us today—truly, concretely, and practically.

What could keep us from celebrating today?

As we celebrate the birth of Jesus Christ, what are we clinging to? Our worries? Our plans for our future? Our fears? Or are we clinging onto the only one whom darkness could not overcome? Are our hearts ready to welcome the son of

God made flesh for us? Do we see the birth of Jesus Christ as a renewed opportunity to trust in God's constancy like Mary did?

Such news fills us with hope and joy. Our savior is here—we no longer walk in darkness.

Feast of the Holy Family

Putting on the perfect bond of love

KERRY WEBER

Sirach 3:2–6, 12–14 or 1 Samuel 1:20–22, 24–28
Psalm 128:1–2, 3, 4–5 or Psalm 84:2–3, 5–6, 9–10
Colossians 3:12–21 or Colossians 3:12–17
Luke 2:41–52

My son's favorite plea these days is for independence. "I will do this by my own," he tells me while climbing the stairs and pulling his hand away from mine. He is not "obeying his parents in everything" as today's reading from Colossians urges, but he is two and a half and so this is to be expected.

And, if I'm honest, the readings for today's Feast of the Holy Family of Jesus, Mary, and Joseph offer several good lessons that I am also too often willing to ignore. There are a number of options for today's readings, but a common thread runs through them all. They tell us that how we treat our family members matters, and then, appropriately, give us some instruction on how to treat each other well.

Some of this advice seems obvious, even if it can be hard to follow: Honor our spouses, honor our parents. Offer one another heartfelt compassion, kindness, humility, gentleness, patience, and forgiveness. As a wife and parent, I'm on board with this.

But some aspects of these readings are tougher sells. I start to feel anxious just reading about Hannah leaving Samuel or about Mary and Joseph frantically searching for the young Jesus. Their experiences remind us that being a parent means engaging in a constant battle between trying to provide the best for our children while simultaneously grappling with all that is out of our control.

My children are the most precious part of my life. I want to keep them close to me; I want to protect them; I want to help them grow to be holy men and women. And so often I think this means making sure that I can orchestrate every detail of their lives so as to shield them from suffering.

But in these readings I am reminded that, although I carried them and birthed them, my children, ultimately, are not my own. They, like Samuel, are dedicated to the Lord. They come from God, and my job is to guide them back to God.

Our readings tell us that there is only one way to manage this. Over all our efforts, all our qualities, we must put on that perfect bond of love. We are asked to think a little less of ourselves; to teach our children to listen and to obey, and then to let them go their own way, even if we don't understand it; to hope that, in spite of whatever anxiety they cause us, we'll find them exactly where they're meant to be; to believe that ultimately we'll be reunited with them in our Father's house.

Another tough sell is that little line in the second reading that I often find troubling—the one about wives being subordinate to their husbands. Yet in the context of the readings for the day I am able to draw something fruitful from it. If we look at the qualities required to fulfill the request rather than at the connotations of the word itself, what is being asked of wives is simply sacrificial love. To love someone means that we are willing to decrease so that another may increase. This is not the same as losing one's sense of self; it's no more than the recognition that we must let go of our own plans and pride in order to encourage others on the shared path of God's mercy before us.

And if this is what it means to love, then a few lines later when husbands are asked to love their wives, maybe the same is being asked of them, just in different words: make yourselves less so that another can be more. In this light, neither partner is being asked to be demurely deferential or a doormat. We're just asked to do what families do, which is sacrifice for each other. We work late nights to support each other; we give up jobs to be with each other; we look away from our screens; we clean up after each other; we laugh; we sit in silence, in sorrow, in solidarity with each other. And we do all this with the aim of modeling the love of Christ, who sacrificed his life for all of us.

There are so many pressures on families these days, and it is all too easy to run around filled with anxiety or bitterness; to provoke each other; to become discouraged. And in our grasping and searching and wandering we long for some feeling of control. But today's readings urge us otherwise: we are asked to let the peace of Christ control our hearts. This means that we must let go of who we thought we were in order to fully become who Christ asks us to be. It means that we must stop insisting we will do things, as my son says, "by our own," and instead recognize that all that we are we owe to the one who keeps reaching out to us, taking our hand, even as we try to pull away—the one who guides us and stands beside us with every step we take.

Solemnity of Mary, Mother of God

Pause and ponder

WAMŪYŪ TERESIA WACHIRA, IBVM

Numbers 6:22–27
Psalm 67:2–3, 5, 6, 8
Galatians 4:4–7
Luke 2:16–21

The feast of the Blessed Virgin Mary, Mother of God is one of the greatest feasts in the church calendar. This is also the day that the whole world celebrates the World Day of Peace: peace in our hearts, in our communities, our churches, our nations, the world.

What a great feast day—let us rejoice and celebrate!

As I prayed and pondered over the readings of this great feast day, three themes stood out for me; the theme of Blessings, Hope, and the Peace of God.

In the first reading, the Lord instructs Moses about blessings, blessings for the Israelites and for us too, because we are the adopted daughters and sons of God through God's Son Jesus, born of Mary.

Be still and let God bless you anew on this day and always. Psalm 67 assures us of these blessings that extend to all the peoples of the earth.

In the second reading, we witness God's great love for us in sending Jesus, born of Mary, to come and dwell among us. This shows how much God loves us and cares for us. Through Jesus's paschal mystery we are no longer slaves but co-heirs with Jesus and children of God who is Abba, our Creator.

The second reading invites us to hold onto this message of hope—that God chose Mary, a woman of humble beginnings, a woman who was lowly in people's eyes, to carry and give birth to Jesus, the Savior of the world, the bridge builder, the bearer of Good News, the one who proclaims the year of God's favor, our true peace, Emmanuel—God with us.

What therefore does it mean for Jesus to dwell among us in our world today?

We live in a world where there is hatred, greed, bad governance, inequality, all forms of violence toward one another and toward the environment; a world splintered by exclusion, especially of those forced to migrate from their countries, those who are different from us. What does it mean for Jesus to dwell in homes and churches that exemplify exclusion, especially of women, at the different tables of fellowship and communion; a world where different forms of abuse whether physical or socio-economic are widespread and rampant? What does it mean for Jesus to dwell in homes and churches where modeling of gospel values no longer appeals to its members? In light of all this, let us pause to consider how we can become a people of hope.

We can start by listening carefully to the gospel reading of today, Luke 2:16–21. This reading tells of an innocent, helpless child lying in a manger, with his mother Mary listening to all that the shepherds are saying of him, keeping all these things and pondering them in her heart.

How often do we listen carefully and ponder these things in our hearts in this busy and materialistic world?

What can we learn from Jesus's lowly and uneventful birth? What can we learn from God's action of choosing a woman whom we in our world would refer to as a nobody, to carry in her womb Jesus—God's loving son? What can we learn from God's choice of shepherds, who are the poorest people in the society, shepherds who smell of sheep to be the first bearers of the Good News?

Let us pause and ponder on this great act of God.

How do I receive those whom I consider irrelevant, a nuisance, those who are different from me, the refugees, the migrants, the poor and marginalized? The Marys and shepherds of our world today.

Today's Alleluia acclamation reminds us that God no longer speaks to us through our ancestors or prophets but through Jesus, God's son. Therefore, let us choose a quiet place and in the silence of our hearts to ponder deeply the message of today's readings. I suggest that we consider the following questions:

Have we paused to ponder in our heart that the poor in our midst is Jesus?

that the migrant risking his or her life at our borders is Jesus?

that the woman whom we exclude from our home and church table of fellowship is Jesus?

that the beggar on our street, with outstretched hand, is Jesus?

that the stranger who does not look like me, does not share my culture, my aspirations, my dream, is Jesus?

that the child lying peacefully in a manger, wrapped in swaddling clothes of poverty, marginalization, homelessness, the most vulnerable member of a desperate family seeking safety, shelter, asylum, is Jesus?

Let us pray and ask God to bless us, to give us the grace to embrace the gospel values, to be bearers of God's Good

News, to be like Mary in bringing Christ to others and especially to our ailing world.

> *God our Creator,*
> *please shine your face upon us,*
> *shine your face on our beautiful world and its people.*
> *God of our salvation, be gracious to us.*
> *Give us true peace so that, like Mary the mother of*
>   *your Son and our Mother,*
> *we may be open to receive your Son Jesus in our hearts*
>   *and in our midst.*
> *Come Lord Jesus,*
> *Emmanuel—God with us,*
> *Come and dwell among us anew*
> *Until we become like you, until we become like you,*
> *Amen.*

Epiphany of the Lord

Traveling toward new horizons

Barbara Quinn, RSCJ

Isaiah 60:1–6
Psalm 72:1–2, 7–8, 10–11, 12–13
Ephesians 3:2–3a, 5–6
Matthew 2:1–12

On this feast of the Epiphany, we do well to step back and see this familiar scene with fresh eyes, letting grace seep into our hearts to enlighten the glorious mystery of the moment. As grace finds its way in, how can we help but exclaim: "This is amazing!" "Can we believe what we are seeing?!"

Shepherds were going about their same old daily work until they unexpectedly came upon a tiny babe and parents who seemed tired, perhaps even terrified, and utterly amazed at the little life before them. Something reminiscent of Isaiah's words in today's first reading echoed in them as their hearts throbbed and overflowed with joy and wonder in the presence of One the likes of whom they had never encountered! In the words of an anonymous believer:

> Blessed are you Christmas Christ
> that your cradle was so low
> that shepherds, poorest and simplest of earthly folk,

could yet kneel beside it,
and look level-eyed into the face of God.

Imagine that! They experienced love like never before—a grounding, empowering, gentle love that said, "You count for something in this world," these poor, simple people who dared not consider themselves important. But they were here and God was visiting them. Their hearts and their worlds would never again be the same.

And then we see the magi, those three sojourning wise men looking for the new king of the Jews, expecting to find one robed in finery, protected by privilege, power, and pride. To their amazement, surprised by grace, they find themselves in the presence of a vulnerable babe whose parents were his only guardians, except for the poor shepherds who were privileged to keep vigil and pay him homage. Can you imagine what was happening in their hearts? The bewilderment, the disorientation, the amazement, the joy? This was hardly what they expected, but it felt so right that their hearts, too, throbbed and overflowed. They were astounded and confounded in the presence of a very different sort of king, one surrounded by rich and poor, wise and unlearned, Jews and Persian gentiles. Was this vulnerable king signaling a new world order, transforming the way things were to what they could become?

These shepherds and wise people were seeing and hearing something that generations before them had never known, as Paul says in our second reading. Newer generations, too, would hear, see, and feel new things in the presence of this vulnerable babe!

Here we are today—a new generation! When the light of the Epiphany star sears our souls, it also casts a beam of light across and beyond any horizon we have previously imagined, calling us to a new vision. Yes, our days are punctuated by normal, everyday common doings, but when we make space for God's grace to inhabit us and soak through to the depths of our hearts, we are amazed and drawn out of our everyday-ness to see and do the unimaginable. God's light will show us amazing possibilities for our world:

- poor and rich, young and old, women and men working together for a more just and more gentle world;
- Jews and Gentiles, yes, but also Muslims, Christians, "nones," and unbelievers recognizing that all of us are on a common journey toward life and love and meaning;
- churches where women and men share equally in the life of worship, discernment, and leadership;
- churches where laity and ordained work as partners and co-creators of communities where all are welcome: people of color speaking in a multitude of languages, gay and straight, married and divorced, those who are searching, those who are lost and forgotten;
- a world of official leaders and common citizens uniting to reverse the climate change that threatens the life of our planet;
- a world where borders that block people from moving toward safety, dignity, and family reunion are dismantled.

Difficult? Yes! Impossible? No . . . not if we let the Light and Spirit of this small and vulnerable babe penetrate our hearts, allowing us to see beyond the darkness of our too-small worlds, the shrunken horizons of our own making. It is not impossible if we are faithful to our everyday calls like the shepherds and ever ready to travel toward new and wider horizons like the wise magi sojourners. It is not impossible if we trust that God teaches us to see to the inside of our daily realities where the power of God is at work, always beckoning us deeper and forward. In the words of William Blake:

> To see a World in a Grain of Sand
> And a Heaven in a Wild Flower,
> Hold Infinity in the palm of your hand
> And Eternity in an hour.
>> (From "Auguries of Innocence")

Let this be our Epiphany prayer.

^

Baptism of the Lord

"I didn't sign up for this"

ANDREA HATTLER BRAMSON

Isaiah 42:1–4, 6–7 or Isaiah 40:1–5, 9–11
Psalm 29:1–2, 3–4, 3, 9–10 or
    Psalm 104:1b–2, 3–4, 24–25, 27–28, 29–30
Acts 10:34–38 or Titus 2:11–14; 3:4–7
Luke 3:15–16, 21–22

In today's gospel we are reminded of the incredible task and daunting responsibility of John the Baptist, the only son of Elizabeth and Zechariah. He lived humbly—wearing his camel hair clothing and leather belt, eating locusts and wild honey, living his vocation to fully preach the coming of one mightier than he.

And then one day it happens. Jesus comes to the banks of the Jordan River. Even then John tries to avoid baptizing Jesus by saying, "I need to be baptized by You, and do You come to me?" But Jesus assures him this is in fact how it MUST be, and then John baptizes Jesus so that Jesus can baptize us in the Holy Spirit. This is why John is here, this is what he does. This is what he signed up for!

I was recently on a pilgrimage that included a meeting with a high-ranking Catholic priest. During our exchanges, among other comments on the state of the Catholic Church, the priest bemoaned the fate and task that had befallen many young priests today. He mentioned how one of his priests had said to him dejectedly, "I didn't sign up for this!" The young priest was lamenting having to deal with the fallout of the horrid sexual abuse scandal that still plagues the Catholic Church.

I confess my first reaction was: "I do not feel sorry for that person. This IS what he signed up for! And if he doesn't think this is what he signed up for, then he signed up for the wrong thing!"

To be sure, many serve in response to a sincere calling, an honest and committed vocation to love the Lord and care for the entirety of the Church. There are people who live with and hear the voices of the poor, the sick, the abandoned, and the abused. This young priest was confronted with hard questions from victims, families, friends, sincere parishioners, all just wanting to know, "Why? How could this happen? How will this be avoided in the future?" And so he wavered—he doubted—"I didn't sign up for this!"

I am a firm believer that everyone will and does waver. We just do. Aw, come on! Even Mother Teresa doubted! We are allowed to—but we go back to our vocations and do our thing!

- How many supervisors have wanted to say after yet another circular conversation about a negative report, "I didn't sign up for this!"

- How many parents of a child with special needs, after cleaning up yet another unintentional mess by a now adult child, have despaired and thought, "I didn't sign up for this!"

- How many children caring for an aging parent who barely resembles the confident, strong parent with whom they grew up, have thought, "I didn't sign up for this!"

- How many parents have buried a soldier-child and cried, "I didn't sign up for this!"

John did everything that was asked of him and then some! All while John's followers were wondering if indeed HE— John—was the messiah. Even as he told them (more than once, I'm sure), "ONE MIGHTIER THAN I IS COMING."

But what if John had just said, "All these people following me, asking me if I am the Messiah!? What if they don't believe me? How can I convince them? What will I do to get this message across? Hmmmm, nah, too much, this is not what I signed up for! I'm out!"

John DID what he signed up for and then some. He preached and baptized.

But even when we think we're doing what we signed up for, life throws us curve balls. Things don't go as planned; they don't work out; things zig when they should have zagged; and we get disheartened. We don't GET what we expected. What DID we sign up for? And what makes us think we can say, "I'm out"?

As Catholics, we were drafted at baptism. Let's be real, we didn't sign up. But WE DID sign up to live Catholic when we received the sacrament of confirmation. That is when we as Catholics receive a special outpouring of the Holy Spirit to increase our ability to practice the Catholic faith in every aspect of our lives. THIS we signed up for! THIS is one of our vocations.

We all waver, we all doubt, we all wonder why us. John wavered before Jesus and then followed through. It is not unreasonable for us to waver, and it is not unreasonable for there to be moments of doubt, anxiety, and fear. But I'll paraphrase the words of the rabbinic sage Hillel the Elder—*If not me who, if not now when?*—words that John the Baptist could have easily used to reference HIS condition.

As you ponder your life, tasks, and responsibilities, let yourself doubt (kinda like John the Baptist), be confident that God accompanies us with love and mercy, and then let yourself stay TRUE to your vocation—whatever it is.

LENT

Ash Wednesday

Giving of myself

CORA MARIE BILLINGS, RSM

Joel 2:12–18
Psalm 51:3–4, 5–6ab, 12–13, 14, 17
2 Corinthians 5:20—6:2
Matthew 6:1–6, 16–18

I'm grateful to be here today and to share with you my thoughts of what Lent is all about. As we celebrate, and as we begin our Lenten journey on Ash Wednesday, I prepared by having three things with me: I had the scriptures for the day, a dictionary, and a book entitled *Black Pearls*, which was written by Eric Copage. It is a collection of daily meditations, affirmations, and inspirations for African Americans. I've been a teacher in the classroom for nineteen years, and therefore I also have homework and you will have homework at the end of this presentation.

When I was a child, I thought as a child. And Lent for me as a child was to give up chocolate ice cream and chocolate candy and chocolate cake. And if it lasted a week, I was lucky. Now I am a woman, so I think as a woman. And as a woman, I know the scriptures and look to them to see what I must do. The readings for Ash Wednesday give me a lot to do. Here I will focus on the fact that in the readings, I see Jesus calling

39

me to be intentional and to be motivational. My second scripture, *Black Pearls*, tells me to also have a purpose; on Ash Wednesday, it says that I need to have purpose.

Looking at the readings, looking at what scripture is saying to me, I see that in these forty days I will be going to be on a journey, and I will take it one day at a time. I feel that doing that will help me to focus and know that I have the graces and blessings of each day. The scriptures also tell us that *today* is the day of salvation. So today—each day of Lent—as I go through it, I will focus on one thing that day.

And the scriptures say a lot about almsgiving. For me, almsgiving is giving every part of my body—my voice, my heart, my lips, my ears. So each day of Lent, I will focus on giving one blessing, one grace that God has given me for that day. One day, it will be that I will speak out against an injustice; another day might be that I will comfort someone who has experienced a death in their family. On another day, it might be that I spend ten minutes with God in silence, trying to see what God is saying to me, being an intentional listener that day. What is God saying to me that day? It might be a time when I will enjoy the whole presence of the beauty of nature that God has given me. Whatever the blessing of that one day is, that will be what I'll focus on. And that will be an almsgiving for that day.

In none of those experiences have I talked about giving money. It has been about giving of myself. And if I do that, then really I am living out and being aware and being intentional about what God wants of me in Lent. And it is something that is not me giving up anything except myself. But it's giving of myself—being positive in what I am doing for the day. And if I do that—if each day I intentionally and purposefully look at something that I am doing, then I will be a real ambassador of God. An ambassador who is a representative of who God is. If I do that, then I will be a true ambassador of what God wants me to be. And, at the end of those forty days, because I have intentionally given myself to God during that time, I will be therefore able to say that I have kept Lent and have purposely been a person who has been an ambassador of Christ.

I invite you during each day of Lent to purposefully, intentionally, really see how you—with your gifts, with the gifts and graces that God has given to you—can also be an ambassador. Then, at the end of those forty days, together we will know that we have been intentionally aware of the real presence of God, that we have given of ourselves and become ambassadors of God. At the feast of the Resurrection we will truly be able to experience the day of salvation and fulfillment. Amen.

First Sunday of Lent

One does not live on bread alone

MELISSA CEDILLO

Deuteronomy 26:4–10
Psalm 91:1–2, 10–11, 12–13, 14–15
Romans 10:8–13
Luke 4:1–13

"The fight is never about grapes or lettuce. It's always about the people." — Cesar Chavez

Cesar Chavez was a farmworker activist and organizer who drew on his Catholic faith to fight for more dignified working conditions for workers on and off the fields.

In today's gospel, when tempted by the devil, Jesus answers, "It is written, One does not live on bread alone."

Jesus and Chavez were two people who knew that to accompany the consumption of our daily food we also need spiritual fulfillment. Sitting at Mass, thinking about the real presence of Jesus in the bread can be overwhelming; to find and feel the real presence of Jesus in communion also takes commitment and prayer.

Similarly, when we consume produce throughout the week it can be hard to remember that real hands picked the crops that we eat daily. It can be hard to recall the interconnectedness we share with our Church body through food.

While not a perfect human being, one of the things Chavez did well that I much admire was always grounding his activism and politics in human dignity. When I read about the way Chavez so often talked about seeing the face of God in each human being, I am reminded of the incarnation, of the way Jesus becomes flesh for us.

This week's readings also remind us to draw on God during our suffering. In today's first reading, it says:

> *When the Egyptians maltreated and oppressed us,*
> *imposing hard labor upon us,*
> *we cried to the LORD, the God of our fathers,*
> *and he heard our cry*
> *and saw our affliction, our toil, and our oppression.*

Affliction, toiling, and oppression are terms used frequently to describe the condition in which farmworkers in this country work. They work through pandemics and wildfires. Hard labor is imposed on them often, regardless of temperature.

Throughout his life, Chavez would use the practice of fasting to promote peace and nonviolence. One of his longest fasts lasted for thirty-six days. Chavez drew on his faith to carry him through these long fasts. He cried to the Lord many times as he fought for something bigger than himself.

As Lent begins, let us remember that we cannot survive on bread alone, just as we cannot on our own produce all the food we need for a happy and full life. Let us remember to lean on Jesus in our fights for justice and in our moments of weakness.

As today's second reading states:

> *For one believes with the heart and so is justified,*
> *and one confesses with the mouth and so is saved.*

Let us remember Chavez and his fasts, his efforts for farmworkers to labor in dignified conditions, for a living wage. During the next forty days, let us think about where our food comes from. Let us also dive deeper into reflecting on our relationship with our daily bread.

Where do we seek nourishment when bread alone is not enough?

How are we inviting God into our fight for justice?

Second Sunday of Lent

God meets us right where we are

SISTER JANE WAKAHIU, LSOSF, PHD

Genesis 15:5–12, 17–18
Psalm 27:1, 7–8, 8–9, 13–14
Philippians 3:17—4:1 or 3:20—4:1
Luke 9:28b–36

Thank you for joining me today as we reflect together on the readings of the Second Sunday of Lent. Once more we are presented with an opportunity to contemplate the love of God for humanity: to deepen our prayer life; to practice fasting, which is a way of denying oneself the excesses of life; and to practice charity and compassion by becoming aware of not only the sufferings of Christ but also the sufferings of others—and reaching out to them in love. Fasting and charity go hand in hand. In this season, plan to give something, however small, to someone in need.

The readings present us with two indispensable episodes. In the Genesis story, God makes a promise to Abraham. "Look up at the sky and count the stars if you can, just so shall your descendants be." Although this extraordinary promise was beyond his imagination, Abraham put his faith in God. At that point, God reveals himself: "I am the LORD who brought you from Ur of the Chaldeans to give you this land of possession."

Like any of us would, Abraham had difficulties fathoming the promise. He asked, "How am I to know that I shall possess it?" God was to show a sign to Abraham; He instructed Abraham to take a series of animals, cut them in two, and lay each half opposite its counterpart. Then, at sunset, a deep sleep fell on Abraham. A significant episode takes place, whereby "a smoking fire pot and a flaming torch passed between those pieces." We see the covenant being sealed with the sacrifice of animals, on the part of Abraham, and a fire, on the part of God.

Think about it, Abraham's encounter with God occurs amidst the ordinariness of his life. So does God speak to us in the ordinariness of our lives—if we dare to listen to him, reflect on his Word, and obediently respond! In the same way, the voice of God speaks to us in the ordinariness of our own lives; how often do we stop to listen?

This segues into the Gospel reading. Luke recounts how Jesus calls three of his disciples together—Peter, James, and John—and leads them to the mountain to pray. This Mountain of Transfiguration has the grace of the Holy Spirit. The Mountain is a holy place of prayer, a place of encounter, a place of revelation. In the presence of the three disciples, Jesus is transfigured! Luke describes, "His face changed in appearance, and his clothing became dazzling white." Two men were conversing with him, Moses and Elijah; they appeared in Glory and spoke of his exodus, which he was to accomplish in Jerusalem. . . . "Then from the cloud came a voice that said, 'This is my chosen Son; listen to him.'"

Both Genesis and Luke's Gospel have three similarities: First, *Revelation.* God reveals Himself to Abraham: "I am the LORD who brought you from Ur of the Chaldeans to give you this land as a possession." And in Luke, God reveals Jesus, "This is My Chosen Son." Second, a *Voice* is heard, with the voice there is communication. "To your descendants I give this land," and in the Gospel, "Listen to Him." Third, the *presence of light*. In Genesis, at sunset, there appeared a smoking fire pot and a flaming torch (a light) which passed between those pieces of sacrificial animals, and in Luke, "Jesus' clothing became dazzling white."

These elements are critical even today. God continues to reveal Himself to us through events and experiences in our lives and through the Scriptures. The Word of God is communicated to us in the Scriptures. How disposed are we to listen to the scriptures, the Word of God, and how do we act on what we hear? During baptism, we are given a live candle signifying light, and we are called upon to be the light of the world. Does our way of life light the way for others?

God's voice exclaimed, "Listen to Him." We are invited to listen to him as he speaks to us in the scriptures and to get out and share our experience with others. A few years ago, while I was taking a walk in the neighborhood, I could not help but hear the arguing of a couple who was having a bad day. I did not know the underlying reason for their argument, but the more they argued, the louder their voices became. I wondered why they are so loud when they are in the same house. They were talking so loudly that they called the neighborhood to hear how angry they were with each other?

Then it dawned on me: neither of them listened to the other. I realized that their hearts were thus separated, and their ears were so blocked by anger that they could not hear each other, regardless of being an inch from each other. God instructs us, "Listen to Him"; do we have any barriers that separate us from each other and God, such that we do not listen to each other or God's Word? To hear the message, we have to be attentive and focused on listening carefully. The seed of the Word of God readily grows in the listener's heart when watered by kindness, endurance, resilience, and support of the community.

The Transfiguration event empowered the disciples to face the difficulties and pain of the cross and to proclaim the message of the Resurrection. The lesson of the Transfiguration is to follow Jesus without fear; he is the way, the truth and the life (Jn 14:6). No matter how difficult the problems may be we should not be discouraged, we should be aware that there is a happy conclusion.

As Jesus took the three disciples to prepare them for his Passion, so too the experiences we are going through could be God flexing our spiritual muscles to prepare us in our journey of faith.

We also learn that words have creative power. The words we use to speak to others can reawaken faith, renew the dreams, and rekindle hope. Through the Word, Abraham received blessings; through the Word, God revealed his Son Jesus to the disciples. God has put potential in us, to use words to encourage; to rekindle faith, hope, and love; to compliment, affirm, and to bless others.

Finally, God meets us right where we are, in the ordinariness of our own lives, but we too have a responsibility to pause, to listen, and to open our eyes to see what God is asking of us. What action do you take? Abraham heard God's promise and responded by laying the sacrifice; the disciples responded by following Jesus and bearing their crosses to the end. What is God asking of you? And how will you respond to the ask?

May this Lenten season be for us a moment of encounter with our God. May we be moved by this encounter to embrace one another with love and compassion!

God bless you.

Third Sunday of Lent
Standing on Holy Ground

KRISTIN HEYER

Exodus 3:1–8a, 13–15
Psalm 103:1–2, 3–4, 6–7, 8, 11
1 Corinthians 10:1–6, 10–12
Luke 13:1–9

God calls us to set the captives free.

Today's first reading from Exodus presents us with an extraordinary image: God appears to Moses in a burning bush, instructing him to remove his sandals, for he is standing on holy ground. Yet it is also a story of God coming to us in our ordinary lives.

Moses is herding his father-in-law's sheep at the time. Imagining Moses leading his flock across the desert reminds me of time spent in the Sonoran Desert in Arizona, here in the United States. The desert landscape is marked by signs of migration: worn-out shoes and empty water bottles dot the unforgiving terrain. Graffiti scrawled on a highway overpass reading "White Pride" sends a clear message to those desperately seeking asylum. Makeshift altars combine recovered clothing, rosaries, and photographs with crosses to commemorate those who have attempted the journey. As a window into the plight of those forced from home, these desert walks have been encounters on holy ground.

We don't have to walk in the desert or witness a miraculous sight to recognize that we are standing on holy ground. As with Moses, God interrupts our ordinary lives as well. We experience moments when something perceptibly shifts and we become aware of the sacred quality of the encounter. As parents, honest conversations with our children about troubling headlines or their own experiences of injustice can bring us onto holy ground. I think of office hours with students, where conversations may start out treating course material, but veer into more meaningful questions about vocation or personal struggle. Perhaps we find ourselves on holy ground when we choose a path that takes courage even when, like Moses, we struggle with real doubts.

While he is tending sheep, Moses leads them beyond the wilderness to Mount Sinai. There he sees fire flaming out of a bush that is not being consumed. Out of this fiery presence, no doubt frightening yet alluring, God comes to him, the perennial outsider. It is Moses—estranged from the Hebrews, a criminal taking refuge—who encounters the God of Abraham, Isaac, and Jacob. God's message to Moses is one of compassionate liberation for those who suffer: "I have heard the cry of my people and come down to rescue them." God calls Moses to go back to Pharaoh and lead the Israelites out of slavery and into the promised land of Canaan. We too are invited to join in this mission of freeing captives for abundant life.

It is in light of the Israelites' own experience of suffering that God frames laws for the treatment of outsiders: "You shall not wrong or oppress a resident alien; for you were aliens in the land of Egypt." Indeed, after the commandment to worship only one God, no moral imperative is repeated more frequently in the Hebrew Scriptures than this command to care for the stranger (the *ger*).*

Across our globe in unprecedented numbers, women, children, and men cross borders. They flee gang violence, food insecurity, and proxy wars. Too often we become numb to statistics or cynical in the face of politicians' manipulative rhetoric. Yet God's clear summons interrupts: Who is crying out in our midst, and what insulates us from their cries? As modern forms of empire continue to exploit, what idols prevent us from showing hospitality? How are our own lives bound up with deaths in the Mediterranean or the Sonoran Desert?

In today's gospel reading from Luke, Jesus reminds us that God's justice is marked not only by liberation but by mercy. His parable of the fig tree reveals how God is patient with us even when we turn away, even when our lives do not immediately appear to bear fruit. The vineyard owner instructs his gardener to cut down the tree because it has not borne fruit in three years. The gardener asks the owner to leave it for one more year, promising to fertilize it, but indicating that the owner can cut it down if it still fails to produce. Lent offers us a time to reflect on the ways in which we must repent and prune in order to grow.

Jesus offers the parable in response to his disciples' questions about the severity of different Galileans' sins. So whereas today's gospel demands we bear fruit, it also warns against

---

*William O'Neill, SJ, "Rights of Passage: The Ethics of Forced Displacement," *Journal of the Society of Christian Ethics* 127:1 (Spring/Summer 2007): 113–36, citing W. Gunther Plaut, "Jewish Ethics and International Migrations," *International Migration Review: Ethics, Migration and Global Stewardship* 30 (Spring 1996): 18–36 at 20–21.

self-righteousness. Sometimes we are more concerned with calling others out than imitating the mercy God shows us again and again. *Why should they exhaust the soil?* Yet responding to God's prophetic call in Exodus often requires the mercy and patience God shows in Luke's gospel—we are called not only to resist empire and release the captives, but also to bridge-build and forgive.

God of one more year, I Am Who Am, you call us to liberating solidarity with those considered "outsiders" in our midst. Together we are standing on Holy Ground.

Fourth Sunday of Lent

Full restoration to the family of God

ANNE CELESTINE ONDIGO, FSJ

Joshua 5:9a, 10–12
Psalm 34:2–3, 4–5, 6–7
2 Corinthians 5:17–21
Luke 15:1–3, 11–32

Can you remember a moment when you were rejected by someone you trusted? Can you imagine returning to your home country from a distant place and being denied access?

Today's readings announce the good news of acceptance where all, irrespective of their dispositions, are eligible for a warm re-entry.

During this Lenten period, eligibility for God's mercy is emphasized as the Church draws its faithful to the penitential nature of the season, to the sacrament of reconciliation, to renewal, penance, and hope. It's an invitation from the merciful Father to an act of sincere contrition, a decisive moment for examining our conscience and returning to the boundless sea of God's love and mercy.

Today's three readings outline the structure of re-entry from sin to grace, from death to life, from being lost to being found, and from indignity to dignity. The first reading depicts the Israelites after God eventually led them to the safety of their cherished ancestral land in Canaan. It was a re-entry from slavery and indignity in Egypt to freedom: a significant moment in their history after years of slavery. Those who arrived celebrated the re-entry to the promised land of plenty.

Similarly, in the gospel, Jesus responds to the question from the Pharisees and scribes about eating with and welcoming sinners by narrating the parable of the two sons and their merciful father. The younger son asks for his inheritance from his father. The father respects his freedom. The son then travels to a far distant country where he squanders it all in a selfish lifestyle. In the midst of his suffering, he recalls how his father treats his servants with dignity. He decides to return home, knowing very well that he has lost his sonship, his inheritance, and his dignity as part of the family. He is hoping to be accepted as a servant.

Meanwhile, the father keeps watching and waiting for the return of his wayward son. The father sees him from afar and is filled with compassion. He runs to embrace him with open arms. He calls for a banquet in his honor. The elder son, unaware of his father's depth of compassionate mercy, sees this and is indignant, saying, "I have been faithful all these years, you have not thrown a party in my honor." He seems to have had a calm spirit before his brother arrived, yet, as the African proverb puts it, "Calm water does not mean there are no crocodiles."

Wise men avow that faults are like a hill; you stand on top of your own and talk about those of other people. The elder brother wants retributive justice applied to his brother—he wants to see some kind of punishment. However, the father's justice is different, because it is based on mercy, love, and the forgiveness that leads to restoration. The father reaches out to the conscience of his elder son, urging him to let go of his selfishness and open himself to the marvel of the re-entry of his lost brother who has returned, a dead brother who is alive, a repentant brother who needs love, mercy, and restoration to the family. Pope Francis's encyclical *Fratelli Tutti* exhorts us to this kind of re-awakening to spiritual brotherliness, sisterliness, to the sense of one family of God, a reconciled human race. In this sense, the father draws the elder son's attention to true repentance and reconciliation, where the old passes away and we are re-created anew.

The gospel challenges us to never lose hope, but like the younger son, to be sorry for our sins, to embrace the father's love, and be spiritually restored back to him. The confession of sin becomes the catalyst for grace; as 1 John 1:8–9 acknowledges, if we say we have no sin we are deceiving ourselves. Consequently, re-entry without repentance does not produce spiritual restoration. It is the acknowledgment of sin that makes possible a renewed change of soul, the type of change that allows grace to transform the spirit. When we are truly contrite of spirit, the conversion experience becomes a divine incarnation filled with the fullness of God, an invitation to intimate communion with Himself and with one another. The Father calls out, "Return to me and I will return to you" (Zec 1:3). "Then, I will restore you" (Jer 15:19). We are called to re-enter the Father's house and have a continuous celebration of every re-entry.

The overhang of the readings provides a methodology of re-entry. Jesus himself powerfully utilizes the parable to offer a spiritual structure of re-entry in a world where re-entry demands retributive justice intended to punish sinners. Within this structure, it is important to know that God is always waiting and watching for the return of the lost. The repentant should recognize their sin and be genuinely willing to turn around. God mediates personally or through others to conscientize those who demand retributive justice to recognize that they too need repentance. The re-entry becomes an unconditional reinstatement filled with festivity and thanksgiving. The imperative for all to be ambassadors of compassionate mercy, mediation, reconciliation, and restorative and distributive justice that leads to full restoration to the family of God—one humanity—is the rationale behind today's readings.

This structure is in consonance with the Synod on Synodality that asks us to reconsider the structures that have long been in place, such as retributive justice for those returning, and evaluate them in the light of the gospel of Jesus Christ. The synod too challenges us to live our faith as ambassadors, lighting the way for others by fostering reconciliation and inclusion where we all come together as one in the beauty of our diversity.

The question remains, which character in this parable would you most identify with at this time? Whatever your answer, plan to re-enter your inner moral conscience during this season of Lent so that we may all join in the celebration of good over evil—the Easter festivity. The good news remains that we are all eligible for God's love, mercy, forgiveness, and transformative restoration.

Fifth Sunday of Lent

Dismantling the structures of shame

TERESA DELGADO

Isaiah 43:16–21
Psalm 126:1–2, 2–3, 4–5, 6
Philippians 3:8–14
John 8:1–11

One of the things that I decided to "give up" for Lent this year was social media. I'm not on Instagram, Snapchat, or TikTok, so that wasn't so difficult, but I was a regular on Twitter and Facebook. My reasons had to do with the way both platforms have become an open invitation for the "take-down," of focusing on one thing, and rallying around a public shaming with the cleverest comeback in 240 characters. Of course, you could use it for staying in touch with family and friends, or learning about breaking news without turning on the television. Still, the temptation to participate in the downward spiral of negativity has often overshadowed its more positive uses, so I just shut it all down.

I share this because I couldn't help but think about the way John's gospel story of the scribes and Pharisees trying to create a "gotcha" moment for Jesus has been read and re-read, interpreted and reinterpreted, as a story only about a woman taken in adultery. This is one of those gospel stories that takes on a life of its own, with elements passed down that aren't in the story, like Jesus writing the sins of all those gathered into the dirt with his finger, when only part of that—Jesus writing in the dirt with his finger—is actually in the text.

I'm struck by the way our interpretive imagination (or lack thereof) has assumed that what the scribes and Pharisees claim is true—this is a woman caught in the act of adultery—and she deserves the shame of being dragged to the temple, placed in the middle of a crowd of people, and condemned to death.

And, based on our belief in that assumption about this unnamed adulterous woman, we have read the story as one of human sinfulness and divine forgiveness, of the grace that transcends judgment and condemnation, a morality tale of what not to do—don't commit adultery, don't condemn others—of "go and sin no more."

I hear something very different in this story.

I'm struck by the timing of the story, not long before Jesus—an innocent man—would be handed over to the Roman authorities on false pretenses, to die a shameful death reserved for the "criminal" in a very public fashion, to terrorize others to stay in their place. He had just spent the night on the Mount of Olives before coming back to the temple in the early morning to teach the people.

I'm struck by the fact that the only ones who accuse the woman of adultery are the men—scribes and Pharisees—who are also trying to use Jesus's response to entrap him. Jesus is the object of their scorn and displeasure; the woman is the objectified means to a calculated end.

What if she were to speak earlier on in the story? Would she say that she had not done what she was accused of doing? Would she have been believed?

She was caught "in the act," but where was her partner who, according to the law, would be condemned to the same death?

As I consider these questions, the story is opened up to us as a radical reimagining of power and privilege, of women's subjectivity against a world of objectification, and of Jesus's accompaniment and solidarity.

In this telling, I can't help but think about the women dragged into the square for a public shaming in our own day, based on assumptions of their sexuality, how women of color, or trans women, for example, are hypersexualized in our society, portrayed in ways that underscore the supremacy and purity of white women to the inferiority and "sinfulness" of Black and brown women's bodies. And the extent our society will go to protect that dichotomy.

In this telling, I can't help but think about women caught in the wars waged by men, used as objects to take other men down in their vying for power. And we know how rape is often used as a weapon of war.

How is it scandalous to say that Jesus enacts no punishment, no condemnation, for an "adulterous" woman, that he just lets her go; yet not scandalous that the religious power structures of the time could have accused an innocent person, condemning her to death, just to prove a point? What responsibility do we have in undoing the systems and structures that make it all too easy to drag a vulnerable person to the middle of the square to be publicly stoned for all to see and participate? Do social media platforms serve as our twenty-first-century public venue where assaults and accusations abound?

I worry that our shame about this story has been misdirected.

As we journey through these final days of Lent, I pray we have not become so desensitized to the harm done by powers and privilege, because we are so much more focused on shaming the "sinner" rather than dismantling the structures that make such shaming all too easy.

The words of Isaiah remind me that God makes possible the seemingly impossible; this is a God who, in the African American spiritual tradition, "makes a way out of no way." Our God refuses to participate in the shaming, objectification, and trickery; our God honors the humanity of those who the world would shame.

The stories of Jesus and the woman accused of adultery are strikingly similar to me. The scandal exists in the manner in which they were treated by men in power, so ready to sacrifice them for the supremacy of their systems, religious and legal. Maybe we, too, are complicit in the scandal if we choose to read from the story only Jesus's response toward a "sinful" woman. In taking a step back, perhaps we can see the scandal of the bigger picture and, without judgment or condemnation, work toward the prize of God's upward calling.

HOLY WEEK

Palm Sunday

Stubborn hope

CECILIA GONZÁLEZ-ANDRIEU

Isaiah 50:4–7
Psalm 22:8–9, 17–18, 19–20, 23–24
Philippians 2:6–11
At Procession with Palms: Luke 19:28–40
At Liturgy of the Word: Luke 22:14—23:56

At this moment, I imagine multiple congregations reflecting on Palm Sunday with me. I can't see you, but I can try to feel you.

The first are my contemporaries, which is why I am wearing this mask. I want to acknowledge that we have lived like this for what feels like a long time. This mark of our limitations has been our reality, a reality of sickness and persistent danger for the most vulnerable, and sometimes violently obstinate denial from others born out of the terrible virus of individualism. So I speak with you as a mother, a caretaker for an elderly parent, a teacher and practitioner of the ministry of theological inquiry and prophetic action. To my contemporaries, especially those responsible for the well-being of others, I want to say: you are not alone in feeling beaten down and close to shutting down your beating heart because it hurts to care. I feel this. Yet, if you are still listening, you are

63

an example of the kind of hope that human beings can generate, when what first appears as an impenetrable darkness engulfs us. In your grief, I am grateful you are here and we are accompanying each other.

The second congregation I imagine are those of you watching this sometime in the future. We have left you our ghosts, images preserved as bits of data. You may have stumbled upon this reflection, a year from now, ten, more. That I believe you are there, somewhere in a future that continues to unfold, is my sign of stubborn hope. You see, as pandemics, wars, and climate change peel off the mask from the world we thought we knew to reveal the wounded reality underneath, many of us are doubting that humanity has any kind of future.

So how do we grab on to stubborn hope right now so you will be there in the future? One way is to look at our scriptures and liturgical year as an intentional training ground for how to meet reality on its terms, transcend it, and then transform it.

But, how do we meet reality on its terms? Palm Sunday's ritual reenactment of events through communal prayer leading into Holy Week provides some answers. Once a year, we are brought into Lent's relentless reminder of fragility and our dependence on God and each other. According to the scriptures, Jesus intentionally walks away from all he knows. He begins a process of shedding the comforts that could dull his senses to seeing deeply into God's heart, or worse, tempt him to look away from the pain crying out to God, co-opted by the promises of power. Only against the starkness of his meeting this reality does Jesus's insistence on endangering his life by going to Jerusalem for Passover make any sense. The reality of his community is there in lives crushed by conspiring powers. He cannot walk away from the offenses against God's desire for radical love, so he must transcend the paralysis that could overtake him and his friends in the face of Rome's brutality and the collusion of the powerful who rely on Rome to prop them up.

The extreme contradiction of his situation is captured in his entry into Jerusalem, where we note the symbolic power of the Mount of Olives. This hill of olive trees beyond the city walls from which Jerusalem comes into view is both the site of the promise of God's reign as he arrives and the site of its most destructive betrayal as he is arrested. The reality is that it is both at once and that this is where Jesus transcends the fear that could stop him, a moment that clarifies for him that violence can no longer be viewed as the answer to conflicts.

And so, we are called out of ourselves to take this road with Jesus, to take up the gift of the reign of God we are called to bring about, while knowing that there will be murderous opposition to that gift. As we step out of our comfort into the starkness of what is real, we transcend fear to see clearly that we must continue on to Jerusalem because that is where change happens. This Holy Week we sit with Jesus in the underground cistern, where he was likely kept overnight as he awaited trial, and try to fathom how it is that he continued to love and work for love in spite of so much evidence that he should just give up. Humanity must have broken his heart. They were hopeless, mired in their own self-preservation, and yet, there were those women, his mother, the Magdalene, the others. Fearlessly they pushed on, wanting him to see them, to know their nearness. As in so many of the stories of his Jewish community, they enacted God's reign, the few who made visible God's love, showing that humanity was not without hope.

Jesus is the last person in history who will die with the question of God's abandonment. Where was God? In his flesh, because he stared down reality and transcended it through stubborn *hope for who we could be*, he forever transformed history. The God of love and of life was indeed present, real, and alive in history, taking Jesus up into God's arms, raising him for all to see: "This, humans, this unstoppable belief in your potential is the key to transformation. Jesus is leading the way, now follow him."

Holy Thursday

Setting the welcome table

KIM R. HARRIS

Exodus 12:1–8, 11–14
Psalm 116:12–13, 15–16bc, 17–18
1 Corinthians 11:23–26
John 13:1–15

I'm Gonna Sit at the Welcome Table

Historic Negro Spiritual and
Civil Rights Movement Freedom Song

[Verse 1 and Refrain]
I'm gonna sit at the welcome table
I'm gonna sit at the welcome table one of these
   days, Hallelujah
I'm gonna sit at the welcome table
I'm gonna sit at the welcome table one of these days

[Verse 2]
I'm gonna walk the streets of glory
I'm gonna walk the streets of glory one of these
   days, hallelujah
I'm gonna walk the streets of glory

I'm gonna walk the streets of glory one of these
    days

[Verse 3]
All God's children gonna sit together (Yes)
All God's children gonna sit together one of these
    days, hallelujah
All God's children gonna sit together,
All of God's children gonna sit together one of these
    days

[Verse 4]
I'm gonna tell God how you treat me (Yes)
I'm gonna tell God how you treat me one of these
    days, hallelujah
I'm gonna tell God how you treat me,
I'm gonna tell God how you treat me one of these
    days

[Verse 5]
I'm gonna sit at Woolworth's lunch counter
I'm gonna sit at Woolworth's lunch counter one of
    these days, hallelujah
I'm gonna sit at Woolworth's lunch counter
I'm gonna sit at Woolworth's lunch counter one of
    these days, hallelujah

[Verse 6]
I'm gonna be a registered voter
I'm gonna be a registered voter one of these days,
    Hallelujah
I'm gonna be a registered voter
I'm gonna be a registered voter one of these days

When I think of Holy Thursday and the eucharistic table, this song always comes to mind.

I see African American college students Ezell A. Blair Jr., Franklin E. McCain, Joseph A. McNeil, and David L. Richmond sitting at the Woolworth's lunch counter in Greensboro, North Carolina, protesting segregation on February 1, 1960. That same year I see courageous college student Diane Nash and seminarian John Lewis leading a wave of sit-ins at lunch counters in Nashville, Tennessee. They connected their faith traditions to their activism and struggle for freedom . . . and the communion table, the eucharistic table, the table where we tell our foundational story for them was also a *freedom table*.

And as I think of those brave young people on this Holy Thursday, I ask all of us this question:

In which direction are we looking?
Are we looking toward freedom?

Are we sitting comfortably and restfully at the table?
Or do we have our shoes on our feet and our
walking sticks in hand, eating like people who are in
flight . . . *ready to create and heed the call, looking*
toward freedom?

I'm gonna sit at the welcome table . . . ready to go.
In which direction are we looking?

Are we looking and bending down, to wash the feet
of a neighbor? Or even allowing our own feet to be
washed in the ritual . . . ? While feeling other than,
feeling above, or even feeling disdain for those who
are in deep need? Unhoused, underfed, unremembered?

Do we see, as we look at our table, not only who is there, but who is not there? Who is not invited? Who is invited but cannot gain access?

All God's children gonna sit together....
In which direction are we looking?

Are we looking up, in adoration of Jesus present in the Eucharist? Are we looking up, yet not remembering, as they say in my community, that God sits on high but looks low. And as we read in the biblical Book of Exodus, God sees and hears the cries and the oppression of the people. And as we know in our own time, God sees and hears the bombs of war and the cries of Her children fleeing for their lives.

I'm gonna tell God how you treat me....
In which direction are we looking?

On this Holy Thursday let us fix our gaze, let us train our attention toward freedom, toward our neighbors near and far off, toward our Savior and our brother, who hears our cries and guides our feet.

We sit at the welcome table,
let us also set a welcoming table ...
and be the ones who expand the welcome with courage.

Good Friday

I thirst for justice

VALERIE D. LEWIS-MOSLEY

Isaiah 52:13—53:12
Psalm 31:2, 6, 12–13, 15–16, 17, 25
Hebrews 4:14–16; 5:7–9
John 18:1—19:42

One of my most cherished religious artifacts is this cross that
I sit before today. It was created for one of the parishes that
I served in as a catechist many years ago. It was also the
parish where I attended Mass while I was in elementary
school. Sacred Heart Church of Jersey City was the Domini-
can Priory for the Order of Preachers. Some years ago, when
the church closed, I was gifted with this cross for my chil-
dren's ministry at Christ the King Church, my home parish.
Christ the King is a historic Black Catholic parish incorpo-
rated in 1930 (ninety-three years ago) in the Archdiocese of
Newark. It was through the initiative of Black Catholic Lay
Women and their families for the Apostolate to the African
American community. My great-grandparents Carrie and
Daniel Livingstone were among those original parishioners.
The mission statement then and now was to seek the right-
eousness of the Lord that all might live in peace. A commit-
ment to social justice, to confront racism and injustice, was

the mission of the parish then and now. You see, the right-eousness of the Lord is justice.

The readings for this Good Friday are engraved on this crucifix from the Gospel of John 19:37. *They shall look upon him whom they have pierced.* Yet it is not just the words but also the imagery of the corpus, the broken and bruised body of our Savior Jesus Christ on the cross that is a central theme for me, not just for today but throughout my life mission. This imagery is foundational and representative of the wisdom and life lessons taught to me by my ancestors of the African Diaspora here in the Americas. Anytime that I would complain or voice disapproval about the injustice shown to me because of my Black skin, my elders would quote the scripture of Isaiah.... *There was no stately bearing to make us look at him, no appearance that would attract us to him, he was spurned and avoided by people...one of those from whom people hide their faces, spurned, and held in no esteem....* After quoting this scripture, my grandmothers, Fleta Lewis and Rachael Livingstone, would say, *"Be thankful that you have not had to suffer death on a cross or a lynching tree."*

My grandparents and ancestors were all born and raised in the South—Georgia, North Carolina, and South Carolina. They knew the indignity of being spurned and hated because of the sin of racism. They experienced being unjustly accused; condemned to endure suffering and degradation. They were not accorded any opportunity to publicly voice a complaint or disapproval of the horrendous oppression. So many parallels to the experiences of the suffering servant spoken of in Isaiah. *"Though he was harshly treated he submitted and opened not his mouth; like a lamb led to slaughter or a sheep before the shearers, he was silent and opened not his mouth. Oppressed and condemned, he was taken away, and who would have thought any more of his destiny?"* (Isa 53:7–8).

Whenever I would ask my grandparents and great-grandparents about their experiences in the Jim Crow South of segregation and the terror of the Ku Klux Klan, their response was *"A burning cross has no power over the Cross of Calvary."* It was their abiding faith and trust in the Blood poured out that day on Calvary that allowed my ancestors and elders the confidence to believe and trust that their help *cometh* from the Lord. *"So, they confidently approach the throne of grace to receive mercy and to find grace for timely help"* (Heb 4:16).

This reliance on the Word of God rested on their awareness that Jesus knew all about their troubles. They knew that they had a Jesus who sympathized with their suffering because he had been tested in every way of suffering. My ancestors saw their own suffering as being linked with the sufferings of Christ on the cross. They knew they would receive the redemptive healing by his stripes and that their suffering would not be in vain.

Their guidance and wise instruction for my journeying through this life of sixty-six years with macro and micro aggressions of racism and injustices was to *"Take courage and be stouthearted and hope in the Lord"* (Ps 27:14). This crucifix that I sit in front of today is a constant reminder of the cost at which my salvation and the salvation of the world was gained.

Standing in the gap with Jesus to the very end were the women—women who stood in solidarity to witness the events so that they could proclaim to the world that a just man was persecuted and put to death for the life of the world.

Can you imagine the hammer hammering? Can you imagine the pain of the crown of thorns, piercing his skull deeper with every blow? Can you imagine the nails tearing into his flesh and bones? That day on Calvary!

Just like the last words, "I thirst!" I thirst for justice. I thirst for the healing of our world from all inequity that has severed the body of Christ—the Church. I believe in the promise of the cross, and I cry out!

In you LORD, I take refuge. In your justice rescue me. (Ps 31:2)

I walk in the promise that by his stripes we are healed. Let the redeemed of the Lord, say so!

EASTER SEASON

Easter Sunday

What needs resurrecting?

KIMBERLY LYMORE

Acts 10:34a, 37–43
Psalm 118:1–2, 16–17, 22–23
Colossians 3:1–4 or 1 Corinthians 5:6b–8
John 20:1–9 (John 20:1–18)

It is hard to believe that in 2022 we are entering the third year of the COVID-19 pandemic. It has been two full years of isolation, illness, and death, especially in our Black and brown communities.

There were times over the last two years that we may have felt despondent, dismayed, and discouraged. More than six million people have lost their lives during this two-year period. It appears that we are now turning the corner and moving out of this deadly period in our history. However, the effects of COVID-19 are ongoing. Economic effects include supply chain shortages and double-digit inflation. Some people are experiencing long COVID, with serious symptoms that can last for months or even years. Everyone is experiencing a little PTSD.

Over the last two years, because of social distancing and other COVID protocols, we have not been able to celebrate the Triduum as we have in years past. While we tried to put on our most happy of faces (behind our masks), it was still different, and we all felt more than a little disconnected.

However, because we are people of faith, we believe in the promises of God that are written in scripture. We believe in the promise of Acts 10 that those who turn away from sin, believe in Christ, fear God, and live righteously will remain in God's love and favor.

In our second reading, Colossians 3 implores us to set our minds on things above. We, who are in Christ, see things from a different perspective. In other words, life in this world will be better if it is lived by focusing on the power of the resurrected, ascended, glorified Christ.

In John's Gospel, Mary Magdalene returns to the tomb and sees that the stone has been rolled away and that the tomb is empty. She panics, runs to tell Peter and the other disciples. When they all return to the tomb, they discover that Jesus's burial garments have been folded in the place where Jesus was laid.

A tomb is a repository for dead people and dead things. This morning my question to you is, "What have you put in a tomb over the last two years that needs resurrecting?" Is it your dreams, which perhaps you now feel too old or unequipped to pursue? Over the last two years some of us may have let fear bury our faith in a tomb. Our peace may have gotten buried in the midst of the chaos happening in our lives. Our self-confidence or self-esteem may have been buried along with our awareness of who we are and whose we are in Christ. Whatever it is that we have buried in the last two years, it is time to resurrect those things.

If we keep reading in this text, we find that Mary Magdalene has an encounter with Jesus. When he calls her by her name, she recognizes his voice. Listen to see if you can hear the voice of Jesus calling your name today. It might be loud and clear, or it might be a still small voice. Today is a reminder that we are a resurrection people who have the power to resurrect those things in our lives that have been buried. Take off your burial clothes and put on your garment of praise. Scripture tells us that God has turned our mourning into dancing. Today is the day we resurrect our dreams, our faith, our peace, whatever it is we have buried.

We are the witnesses in today's world of the resurrected Christ. This is the day that the Lord has made. Let us rejoice and be glad. Go and tell everyone you encounter, Jesus is alive.

Second Sunday of Easter

Touching the Resurrection

NOELLA DE SOUZA, MCJ

Acts 5:12–16
Psalm 118:2–4, 13–15, 22–24
Revelation 1:9–11a, 12–13, 17–19
John 20:19–31

The gospel for this Second Sunday of Easter is about the skeptical, cynical, and unbelieving realist called Thomas. He is there to help us capture the presence of the Resurrected in our midst today. The community tells Thomas of their experience: "We have seen the Lord," but Thomas responds, "Unless I see the nail holes in his hands, put my finger in the nail holes, and stick my hand in his side, I won't believe it."

For Thomas, things could not be otherwise than how they are. He is a prototype of pragmatic thought. Things cannot change, because there is a long history of failures and disappointments. In fact, Thomas's senses have been hardened.

But what Jesus asks of us is that you and I open up to a new dimension. When he gives us the gift of faith and we welcome it, we discover that reality is inhabited by a presence filled with unsuspected possibilities. We do not have to see in order to believe, but we need to believe in order to see.

When we touch the Resurrected in today's crucified, we touch the wounds of those whom our system tries to make invisible, we admit, like Thomas: "My Lord and my God!"

Reading the Gospel of John, we ask for that grace that we may touch and be touched by—that we feel interiorly—the depth of suffering there is in the world today, symbolized by Jesus's passion, suffering, and death. We ask for the courage to follow in the footsteps of Jesus in life, in the Church, in the world, an experience that is always of humility, oftentimes made possible only through the eyes of faith.

Like Thomas, we travel with faith and hope, not vision. We continue searching for him and we realize the Resurrected is already around us. If we do not have faith, we cannot detect signs of the Resurrection. They are sometimes subtle and small, like the mystery that surrounds a seed, something so seemingly simple, something without a shine. We have the capacity to detect these signs of the Resurrection, even in the midst of pain.

So how do we live this communion of the resurrected in the crucified? How do we touch his wounds in our system, and yet be with the Resurrected?

There are four elements in any Easter story we could look for:

1. Expect the resurrected in the unexpected . . . in our simple, everyday life.

2. Jesus is with the living, not with the dead. Wherever there is a cry for life, he is there. In the uprisings in the different parts of the country against domestic violence, he is there.

3. The Resurrected Christ offers us life, and as his followers we continue fighting for a better life for

everyone, struggling for equality for all human beings and respect for all.

4. We are asked to reflect regularly and practice our faith in the Resurrection...to spend some time each day detecting its signs in our daily life.

For this, we need only to have an attitude of reverence and respect for all. We need to commit ourselves to the invitation to share the vision of Jesus and be his companions.

If the Resurrection is Christianity's defining moment, it is also the moment that brings into question the different ways the Christian Church as an institution has traditionally treated women. In this regard, the patriarchal foundation of the Resurrection story is obvious. Although the wind is blowing in the direction of inclusivity, the forces of patriarchy within the universal church still holds sway, and it will take some time before the events of that first Easter Sunday make a difference in the way women are treated not just in the Catholic Church but within the wider Christian family. But remember, women were the first communicators of the Resurrection story—even in our own context of patriarchy and hierarchy—we still are.

Yes, we women are the wounded, sharers in the crucifixion of today. But I prefer to see us in our power, bearers of Good News with the ability to touch the fragility of the Resurrection today.

And so, when women refuse to assume the dehumanizing values of a patriarchal society and propose with their lives another way of being and relating, we touch the Resurrection.

When a woman breaks the circle of submission and violence, when she dries her tears and lifts her head, we touch the Resurrection.

When women unite in order to look for paths for united solutions, join together in order to change situations of pain and suffering and open doors to abundant life, we touch the Resurrection.

When women study and get ready to overcome discomfort, mistrust, prohibitions, and complexities, we touch the Resurrection.

No small attempt made to improve the lives of those who are discounted or oppressed gets lost in a vacuum, and we have seen this time and again.

And yes, women are rising—from our silence, bondage, exclusion, exploitation—we are rising into hope, freedom, speech, power, partnership, significance. We are rising into the future.

In conclusion, we ask You, Holy Spirit, to pour on us the gift of counsel, so that we may learn to accompany others. Make us present where there is pain and suffering. Inspire us with your words of encouragement and hope, that with our actions and our words we may be signs of your loving presence.

Third Sunday of Easter

We are not stuck

Mary Kate Holman

Acts 5:27–32, 40b–41
Psalm 30:2, 4, 5–6, 11–12, 13
Revelation 5:11–14
John 21:1–19

The Easter season is upon us. It is a time that is meant to be joyful and hopeful. For some of us, though, joy and hope may feel hard to come by these days. Whether we are suffering from personal hardship or struggling with the pain of injustice and abuse in our church, it may be hard to enter into a spirit of "good news."

Even our gospel readings these past few weeks show us the first witnesses of the Resurrection filled with discomfort and uncertainty. For Mary Magdalene, the encounter with the risen Jesus brought about confusion; for Thomas, news of the Resurrection brought about doubt. In each of these stories, Jesus's friends and disciples are still reeling from the *trauma* of seeing their friend and teacher executed, the *grief* of losing him, the *fear* of being persecuted as his followers, and the *shock* of learning that he has risen from the dead. They're not sure what this resurrection means for them.

This is particularly true for Peter, the main figure of today's gospel passage. On Good Friday, he denied Jesus . . . three times. Now Jesus is back—certainly good news—but where does that leave Peter? And where does it leave us?

Peter announces that he's going fishing, and the others choose to join him. They spend all night in the boat—and catch nothing. We aren't told if they keep casting their nets unsuccessfully, or if they simply leave them out and wait. But either way—no fish. Perhaps this feeling is familiar to us, the feeling of trying or waiting for long stretches of time, with nothing to show for it. Paralyzed by grief, stubbornness, or inaction. Stuck.

But then Jesus appears on the shore, unrecognized by the disciples. He suggests that they try something new—cast the net over the right side of the boat. Immediately, the haul of fish is overwhelming. From emptiness to abundance. Our first glimpse of good news—the resurrected Jesus offers a new way of seeing things, a new way of doing things. We are not stuck.

Peter doesn't realize that it's Jesus until the beloved disciple tells him. Peter is obviously not the most perceptive, nor the one with all the answers. And here's my favorite moment, where we see Peter at his best: As soon as he DOES learn that it's Jesus, he throws on some clothes, leaps into the sea, and swims to shore as fast as he can to meet Jesus. He can't even wait for the boat to make it the short distance to shore—he is bold, and joyful, and totally open to Jesus's invitation. And then to hear an invitation to a loving, intimate meal among disciples—"Come, have breakfast." More good news—community is restored.

Jesus addresses Peter's worst fear head on. Remember the denial? Now Jesus asks him three times: "Do you love me?" And with each response of "Yes, Lord, you know I love you," Jesus responds: "Feed my lambs. Tend my sheep. Feed my sheep."

We hear that Peter is "distressed" when Jesus asks a third time. Perhaps he's feeling defensive. None of us like to be reminded of our failures, the times we were at our worst. But Jesus does not hold Peter in that place of shame. He also doesn't pretend that the denial didn't happen. I think this is perhaps the most important good news of all. Jesus invites Peter to new life in the exact place of his greatest failure. And that's how resurrection works.

We've seen the ways that the figure of Peter, the "rock" on whom Jesus builds his Church, has been misused in some Catholic circles: to encourage blind deference to authority, to perpetuate exclusionary practices, and to make excuses for incompetent leadership. We've seen those who claim their authority in direct lineage from Peter continue to deny Jesus out of some combination of self-preservation and terror. This is a distortion of the Gospel—it is not good news, and it has not borne good fruit. It is an utter rejection of Jesus's command, "Feed my lambs."

But today's reading from John IS good news because it can empower us. The risen Jesus sets Peter free from his shame by tasking him with the concrete care of his lambs.

Where can we as Church heed Jesus's invitation to cast our nets differently when our present practices aren't working? Where can we joyfully, boldly rush out to meet Jesus on the shore? How can we call our Church to repent of our shameful denial of Jesus, and, in an affirmation of our love for him, feed his sheep?

The good news of the Resurrection isn't something that we receive passively; it is God calling us to action. The hope and joy of the Easter season come from our realization that we are not stuck. Jesus sets us free so that we can share in his work: feeding his lambs and proclaiming the Resurrection to a hungry world.

Fourth Sunday of Easter

We are all sheep

Colleen Gibson, SSJ

Acts 13:14, 43–52
Psalm 100:1–2, 3, 5
Revelation 7:9, 14b–17
John 10:27–30

A few years ago, when the neighborhood center at which I currently minister was just a dream, a group of sisters set out to find a physical space for the project to call home. Having served in the city of Camden for more than 150 years, our sisters began by visiting parishes that they thought might be willing to partner with us or that had empty properties our congregation could rent. Their dream was to open a center where neighbors could meet and grow in community and people from throughout the city and suburbs could come together for opportunities of connection, enrichment, and empowerment.

As the sisters met with pastors and described their vision of a beloved community, their message was met with regrets, citing inadequate capabilities; hopes that more profitable plans would come along; and reservations about a vision that the pastors couldn't quite comprehend. Time and again, the sisters left meetings with hopes that maybe the next appointment would offer more promise.

After many months, and having visited all the prospective parishes in the area, the sisters finally faced the fact that their message wasn't getting through. The mandate for the neighborhood center had come from a Congregational Chapter and so, we believe, was dictated by the Holy Spirit.

Filled with that Spirit and shaking the dust from their feet, the sisters set out once more. This time they searched far and wide, looking deep into the heart of the communities they wished to serve. In time, they came upon a little Lutheran church a few blocks from a once-wished-for site at a Catholic church. The congregation of the Lutheran church was small—maybe twenty-five people on a good Sunday—but they were intrigued by the plan the sisters set forth and were willing to rent their old Sunday-school building to the sisters so that they could give it a shot. As the pastor would come to say, "We're all just trying to live out the same Good News."

Reflecting on today's readings, I'm amazed at how Good News speaks to each of us. One of the things I love about the Easter season is the way in which our readings put into context the call of Christian discipleship. Jesus says in today's gospel, "My sheep hear my voice; I know them, and they follow me." These beautiful words from the tenth chapter of John's Gospel come in response to the pressing question of whether Jesus is the Messiah. "Tell us plainly" (John 10:24), the people demand in the lines right before today's reading. "I told you and you do not believe," Jesus replies before going on to speak about how his sheep know his voice and follow him.

Like good sheep, Paul and Barnabas show us the way of their shepherd in action. When they declare the word of God to the Jews, their message comes in two parts. First, they tell those who hear and believe to "remain faithful to the grace of God." To those who object to their manner and message, they boldly declare that they will then speak to those who will hear them. This delights the Gentiles who are eager to hear and take up the gospel message.

In an age when division runs rampant, though, I am cautious of the way today's readings, or even my own story, could be interpreted. A cursory glance might easily lead to drawing party lines, creating an us-versus-them narrative. Nothing could be further from the Truth of the gospel.

As the psalmist sings: "We are God's people, the sheep of his flock." God knows us and loves us, even when we don't hear so well. At a moment in our church and our world when people have stopped listening to one another or are selectively listening to the voices they agree with, we must remember—no one is greater than the others—we are all sheep.

Created in the image and likeness of the Lamb, we are called to follow him wherever he leads. To do this, we must remain faithful to the grace of God, acting as instruments of salvation, striving for justice, and allowing joy and the Holy Spirit to be pervasively present in all we do.

The Easter season is one of rejoicing. Jesus is risen! The Good News dwells among us! Despite times of great distress and division, God has a vision for our world. It is a vision of a world in which every nation, race, people, and tongue are united. It is a vision looking for a home in our hearts; it begs us to listen, and I pray that, in this Easter season and in all the seasons of our lives, we might live faithfully enough to bring it to birth.

Fifth Sunday of Easter

What does it mean to be a disciple?

MELINDA BROWN DONOVAN

Acts 14:21–27
Psalm 145:8–9, 10–11, 12–13
Revelation 21:1–5a
John 13:31–33a, 34–35

What does it mean to be a disciple? This is the question that today's scripture readings invite us to ponder.

In the Acts of the Apostles, we see Paul and Barnabas as partners on mission: men on the move, traveling widely to spread the gospel. Apprenticed to the very person of Jesus, they are committed to a way of life. From this narrative, we learn that being a disciple means telling the sacred story, encouraging each other, appointing leaders, and gathering as a community in prayer and fasting.

Paul and Barnabas did not sugarcoat the calling to follow Jesus. Instead, they named the reality of hardship and struggle, ever-present in the face of resistance and danger. How are WE, as followers of Christ, urged to persevere, to stay the course, not only in encountering outward resistance but when wrestling with the resistance in our own hearts?

The vision of John in the Book of Revelation is a message of great hope and assurance for discipleship: we are not alone.

God *dwells with* us, accompanies us. The Holy One, who wipes away every tear, transforms suffering and discouragement, and indeed, makes all things new.

God's creation did not happen only once in the beginning, to remain static for all time. Rather, God *is creating* here and now, continually, in an ongoing way. We need only look to the seasons of nature to see this ever-changing creative activity.

In today's gospel reading, Jesus is offering his last will and testament; a scene that falls between the sharing of the Last Supper and foot washing, and the betrayal and arrest of Jesus. Knowing that his time is short, Jesus tenderly addresses the disciples as "My children." He voices the one thing that was most important for them to hold onto, saying, "I give you a new commandment: love one another."

Loving one's neighbor was not new to these faithful Jews. What *was* new, was that this instruction was on the lips of Jesus, and he made it very personal, saying: "As *I* have loved you, so you should also love one another. This is how all will know that you are my disciples, if you have love for one another." He was lifting up his own time on earth as their model for discipleship.

How had he loved them? This carpenter from Nazareth healed the sick, the blind, and the lame. He shared table fellowship with the hated tax collectors, and he forgave sinners. He fed the multitude, grieved with mourners, and raised the dead. He reached out to the least and the lost, and welcomed all with open arms. In the supreme act of servant love, he cradled and washed their dusty feet, and he sacrificed his life on the cross, for them and for us.

What does it mean to be a disciple? When my mother died, a friend wrote, "You will keep her memory alive by living into her virtues." It was the most consoling and yet the most challenging thing anyone could have said. It was consoling because my mother had been a person of great virtue, and here was a concrete way to hold onto her legacy.

I could *do* the things she did, support the causes she held dear, but living into her virtues required more. It required me to *be* in a new way. It required me to live with greater intentionality, to live into the purity of my mother's generous, Christ-like love. She received all without judgment, and this was mine to live into. Mom was the one who could forgive anything and ask for forgiveness. She was the one who reached out to those who were sidelined on the margins, and the one who lived social and religious tolerance from the core of her being. As she did, so must I.

What does it mean to be a disciple? It means that we must love one another with all that we are, because *how* we live into the love of Jesus is what defines us as his own. As receivers of that redemptive love, we are called to *embody* the love of Christ: to become a community of healing mercy, kindness, inclusion, compassion, and forgiveness.

Being a disciple means that we hold Jesus and each other close. It means that we hold, with confident trust, the truth that God can and does and will make all things new.

Sixth Sunday of Easter

It is good that God is here

M. PATRICIA BALL

Acts 15:1–2, 22–29
Psalm 67:2–3, 5, 6, 8
Revelation 21:10–14, 22–23
John 14:23–29

Peace I leave with you. My peace I give to you.

Wow!

Don't we yearn for this right now?

In a world beset with conflict and division, pandemic and sorrow, is it not tempting to give up on finding peace?

Maybe we are looking in the wrong place for peace.

In today's reading from the Acts of the Apostles, we learn that, even in the early church, there was dissension caused by the spread of misinformation by unauthorized messengers.

Sound familiar?

In response to this, Paul sent his trusted messengers to allay the concerns of the Gentiles who were anxious about whether they needed to follow Jewish law in order to be followers of Christ. Specifically, the men were worried about whether they needed to be circumcised. Paul was clear, though, that the message he was sending came through the Holy Spirit, God's presence among them.

In our parish last year the liturgy committee decided on a theme for the year: "It is good that we are here." As we pondered that statement, we wondered what the congregation might think. After all, we were in the midst of a pandemic.

We know that times were also very treacherous for the early Christians. Daily they were threatened with persecution. Those threats consumed their daily thoughts and activities and yet was it not good that they were there?

God did not promise any of us a smooth road. Maybe it is in times of deep discord and peril that the beauty of Christ's teaching can best be seen.

Following on last year's theme, this year our liturgy committee chose as our theme, "It is good that *God* is here." While we also can find a challenge in believing *that* to be true in the midst of turmoil, it is just this fact that brings us hope and comfort.

In today's gospel passage, Jesus tells the apostles that he will be leaving soon. That doesn't sound very comforting.

How terrifying that must have been for His apostles. After all, they had been with him day and night for the previous three years. They ate with him, they laughed with him, they prayed with him, they probably even danced with him. They grew to know him and to love him, this Messiah for whom their ancestors had been waiting for generations. He had been their teacher in word and deed. I think we have all had the experience of hearing the almost unbearable news that we were going to lose a loved one, a friend, a mentor. How, we wonder, can we go on? How can we continue their legacy? For all its intensity, a three-year period is not a significant part of a lifetime, and the apostles were expected to spread his good news far and wide? They were to build his Church? These were fishermen, tax collectors, craftsmen, and not necessarily the most educated bunch. These were men and women who repeatedly erred even to the point of denying knowing Jesus immediately prior to his death.

Still there is some comfort in this same gospel passage. Jesus reminded the apostles that he would return soon. More importantly, he, as with our loved ones and friends, would always be with them and us in what they had permanently implanted in our hearts and souls.

It is good that God is here.

Jesus further said to his disciples: "*Whoever loves me will keep my word, and my Father will love him, and we will come to him and make our dwelling with him.*"

How many of us start our day with the prayer that goes something like this, "My God, I offer you all my thoughts, words, and deeds of this day"? I know that at times I have considered saying this to be justification for how I lived God's word and prayed unceasingly as Paul urged us to do.

At the end of some days, though, I wonder how many of those thoughts, words, and deeds I am proud of. I, like the apostles, fail to preach the gospel through my actions. I do find comfort, however, in believing that God has been by my side throughout the day and still loves me. Amazing!

I also take comfort in the words of Richard Rohr, when he says, "For Jesus, prayer seems to be a matter of *waiting in love. Prayer isn't primarily words; it's primarily an attitude, a stance, a modus operandi.*" We can pray unceasingly and live the gospel if we find sustenance in remembering that we are engulfed in God's loving embrace. In that embrace we can find the peace he gives and that we so desire.

It is good that God is here.

Solemnity of the Ascension

Embracing newness

GRETCHEN CROWDER

Acts 1:1–11
Psalm 47:2–3, 6–7, 8–9
Ephesians 1:17–23 or Hebrews 9:24–28; 10:19–23
Luke 24:46–53

A few weeks ago, during Holy Week, my son had a Stations of the Cross performance at school. Each of the classes took a station, and his kindergarten class was assigned #14, "The Burial of the Lord." His role was simple—he just had to kneel on one of the steps of the altar, put his face into his hands, and mourn the death of the Lord. There were no lines, no significant body movements or hand gestures. But, as I watched him walk with his class to the foot of the altar, kneel down, and cover his face with his hands, I was awestruck.

Just a little over a year ago, my son had undiagnosed hearing loss. For years, he had struggled to communicate with us, and we had struggled to understand him. And when asked to do anything in front of anybody, he would fold his arms, purse his lips, and refuse. Or sometimes, locked in confusion at what he was being asked to do, he would cry and scream. Unsure of what to do, since many doctors and speech therapists had told us our suspicion of hearing loss was false, I figured perhaps he was just shy. So, I would try and encourage (and sometimes drag him) onto the soccer field or persuade him to say hello to people and just be polite. Nothing worked. A year ago, before we finally understood what was wrong, if I had to imagine my son going up with his class to the altar in front of hundreds of people and doing exactly what was asked—I would have said, "Never gonna happen."

As a parent, or honestly just as a human being, when we are in a challenging season, it is so difficult to see an end in sight. Particularly when we are tired or worn down or just trying to keep everything together...

We can often feel like this particular period will never end.

I was "in the weeds" (as they say) for years, trying to navigate and understand my son with no true comprehension of why it was all so difficult. There were many moments when I sat and cried, mourned a loss for which I had no name, and asked God to please take this confusion and suffering away.

In today's first reading, the apostles have many questions for the Lord. They are about to be "in the weeds" themselves as their friend and mentor will have left. They want to know what will happen and how they will handle all of it. But the Lord replies, "It is not for you to know the times or the seasons." He explains that they will receive the power of the Holy Spirit and be given all the tools they will need in order to carry on the work in his absence. Still, as he departs from them, they remain staring up at the sky—possibly still waiting for direct answers, possibly waiting for someone to take away their confusion and suffering over the death of their friend. The first reading ends with two men in white garments asking them to lower their eyes and move forward in faith.

The second reading of Paul to the Ephesians continues this message of looking forward with hope. He says, "May the God of our Lord Jesus Christ, the Father of glory, give you a Spirit of wisdom and revelation resulting in knowledge of him." Paul prays that they may have hope and trust in the One who has power over all things of this earth. He invites them to see beyond their limited vision and believe.

Belief is easier with reminders of God's presence, though, isn't it? In the gospel, the disciples hear from the Lord once again. He reminds them of his victory over death, and he blesses them. Having an encounter with Christ allows them to return to Jerusalem "with great joy," praising God. When I went to my son's kindergarten class to pick him up after the Stations, his teacher leaned down and hugged him and said, "I am SO proud of you! You weren't shy, you didn't hesitate! You were brave! It was incredible!" She, too, has been a witness to the Resurrection inside my son.

As two bright blue hearing aids now adorn his ears, his world has opened up to all the possibilities around him. At first, he was hesitant, dipping his toe in the water as he experienced new sounds and interactions with people. He took his time adjusting to a world he had not previously known. And as he explored and learned and gingerly tried one new thing after another, we all got to witness Christ moving in him.

There is another thing I realized recently about this Christ moving inside of him—this new child who is more fully himself than ever before: he is very different from the child I first knew. As a parent, a wife, a sister, a friend . . . it is sometimes incredibly difficult to navigate change in another person. To be able to remove the lens of the person you have known and see instead someone anew. And not only see someone anew, but embrace the newness in them, and not linger on what has passed.

The disciples post-resurrection have something very important to realize about their friend Jesus . . . and perhaps this realization is difficult to wrap their minds around—their old friend has passed away. Jesus as they knew him has died and he will never be the same again. He is not less special, he is not less their friend, not less in love with each one of them...but he is something *completely new*. And at this moment, if the disciples fail to recognize this newness, if they dwell on what has passed, they might miss so much ahead that is truly special. If they continue to raise their eyes up to heaven instead of looking forward to the Christ in their midst, they will miss the point.

It is difficult for me, sometimes, to not respond to my son in the old ways. It is difficult for me to not just assume he will be shy or he will fail to respond to others or that a misunderstanding won't result in hours of crying and screaming on both our parts. I am continuously trying to grow and change in my approach to him and the wonderful person he is and the wonderful person he is becoming. I know that if I fail to notice him as a continual creation of God, if I keep my eyes focused on what was instead of what is, I will miss that glimpse of Christ right in front of my eyes.

I pray that we all are given the grace to look into the eyes and faces of those around us and witness Christ alive in each encounter.

Pentecost

The dwelling place of Spirit God Different

M. SHAWN COPELAND

Acts 2:1–11
Psalm 104:1, 24, 29–30, 31, 34
1 Corinthians 12:3b–7, 12–13 or Rom 8:8–17
John 20:19–23 or John 14:15–16, 23b–26

The socially constructed and sanctioned oppression of children, women, and men *in* and *because* of embodied or fleshly difference continues to re-emerge as the urgent issue of our time. This predicament constitutes a challenge to Christian discipleship.

Consider that COVID-19 and its variants continue to inflict great suffering, bringing together the peoples of our planet in a tragic solidarity of suffering, death, and loss. At the same time, the dynamics and conflicts of neoliberal capitalism continue to throw us all into a common geo-political space that homogenizes and suppresses us, pits us against one another.*

---

*Anselm Min, *The Solidarity of Others in a Divided World: A Postmodern Theology after Postmodernism* (New York: T & T Clark, 2004), 93.

The sharpening of the ecological crisis radically clarifies humanity's fundamental unity *in* difference and raises the stakes for the ongoing survival and life of *all* species, including our own. Consider that North Korea's insistence on testing nuclear weapons and Russia's unprovoked war against Ukraine only intensify geo-political division and hostility. Consider our own American moral and intellectual ignorance about the meaning and function of our republic. Consider that our debased practices of kyriarchy and white supremacy continue to sow arrogance and hatred among us through imperious misogyny, disdain for homeless women and men, disregard for Indigenous peoples, condescension toward differently abled women and men, dismissive attitudes toward massive rates of incarceration, contemptuousness toward immigrants and asylum seekers, normalization of "white privilege," and mass shootings of LGBTQI persons, Asians, Blacks, Jews, immigrants, Latinos, and other people of color. Through apathy and silence, indifference and mindlessness, we incriminate ourselves in the oppression of those who are Jesus's brothers and sisters—those whom we have made "least" and "wretched."

Yet, oppression as perpetrated by those who wield power with brute force or cunning coercion "betrays their fear that another power, other than theirs and greater, has been unleashed."* What *is* that greater power? *Ruah.* The Hebrew word *ruah* is translated in the New Testament as the Greek word *pneuma,* meaning breath, air, wind, or soul. In Hebrew, *ruah* denotes spirit, breath, wind and is almost always connected with the life-giving attribute of God. Spirit-*ruah* is and remains paradoxical, elusive, uncontrollable, absolutely

---

*Bernard Cooke, *Power and the Spirit of God: Toward an Experience-Based Pneumatology* (Oxford: Oxford University, 2004), 26–27.

free. *The Spirit, like the wind, blows where and when and how the Spirit so chooses* (after John 3:8).

The French theologian Louis-Marie Chauvet suggests that "The Spirit *is* God Different.... [A]t the same time, [the Spirit] is God closest to humankind, to the point of inscribing God's very self into our corporality in order to divinize it."* If *Spirit God Different* inscribes the Divine Self into (or divinizes) our human bodies, integrates and embraces all God's human creatures, then affirmation and embrace of embodied or fleshly human difference *is* the mission of *Spirit God Different*. Indeed, from the beginning, *Spirit God Different* moves among all God's human creatures—drawing us together, inspiring, prompting, prodding, exhorting, reproving, animating, empowering us to defy disunity and division, rupture and separation.

At Pentecost, *Spirit God Different* publicly performs and ratifies the Triune God's respect and love of our embodied, fleshly human differences. At Pentecost, *Spirit God Different* missions *us* to live out the command of Jesus to "love one another." *Spirit God Different* opens us, teaches us to live in and live out active compassionate, loving solidarity with those whom our society chooses to oppress—those whom our society exploits and alienates, marginalizes and dominates, rejects and denies, attacks and assaults, represses and crushes, murders and destroys. By creating these blessed fleshly differences, *Spirit God Different* nudges us to reach out to one another, to communicate, to meet one another, to enjoy one another, to act in love for and with one another. *Spirit God Different* urges us to defend and protect one an-

---

*Louis-Marie Chauvet, *Symbol and Sacrament: A Sacramental Reinterpretation of Christian Existence*, trans. by Patrick Madigan and Madeline Beaumont (Collegeville, MN: The Liturgical Press, 1987/1995), 518, 522 (author's italics).

other from oppression and violence of body and soul, mind and heart; to respect and honor, welcome and embrace one another in all our fleshly difference—for our shining and beautiful fleshly differing bodies are dwelling places of *Spirit God Different.*

ORDINARY TIME

Second Sunday in Ordinary Time

Reflecting God's glory

JANE E. REGAN

Isaiah 62:1–5
Psalm 96:1–2, 2–3, 7–8, 9–10
1 Corinthians 12:4–11
John 2:1–11

The gospel for this Second Sunday in Ordinary Time brings us back to the beginning of Jesus's public life with the story of the wedding at Cana, the first public miracle or sign, as John calls them.

There are a number of questions to get tangled up with in this story. Like how come those hosting the celebration ran out of wine? How did Mary find out about it? And the interchange between Jesus and his mother Mary raises an eyebrow. Mary makes an observation: they have run out of wine. Whether it was her tone of voice or the look in her eyes, Jesus got that she expected him to do something about it. His response reminds me of the look I get from my young-adult daughter when I remind her that the dog needs a walk or that there is garbage that could be taken out. "How does your concern affect me? My hour has not yet come." With classically good parenting skills, Mary avoids getting caught up in the argument, and simply tells the attendants to do what Jesus says.

And we know how it ends, with six large jars of water now wine, indeed the best wine. And the wedding party saved.

But there is a final sentence in the story that is key to understanding it and fruitful for our own reflections. John writes: "Jesus did this as the beginning of his signs at Cana in Galilee and so revealed his glory, and his disciples began to believe in him."

"And so revealed his glory, and his disciples began to believe in him." This is a theme in John's Gospel—the notion of glory and that the signs that Jesus performed revealed Jesus's glory, a glory that is participating in the glory of God. Jesus's act of kindness, his responding to a family in need, glorified God and led his disciples to begin to believe in him.

The idea that the glory of God is dynamic and expansive can be found in our Old Testament reading as well. At this point in Isaiah, the Israelites' time in exile is over. They have returned to their own land as a people God has freed. Through this action Israel is led out of bondage and, as Isaiah writes, "Nations shall behold your vindication, and all the kings your glory." As in the gospel, it is the action of God that brings glory to Israel—a glory that reflects the gracious glory of God.

Now, we could do a word study on the use of the word "glory" in John's Gospel or in Isaiah, but the more important theological question we ask: So what? So what does this mean for how I live my life, raise my children, spend my money—how I live my faith? Let me propose three points to reflect on:

First, the reading from Isaiah highlights the saving, liberating action of God through which the glory of Israel and ultimately the glory of God is revealed. The writer of this section of Isaiah says:

No more shall people call you "Forsaken,"
or your land "Desolate,"
but you shall be called "My Delight,"
and your land "Espoused."

What struck me is how important it is that the Israelites accepted the new naming. They had experienced themselves as forsaken and desolate for so long that fully embracing this new reality could well be a challenge. The challenge for us is similar. How well do we embrace the notion of ourselves as beloved of God, as people who reveal God's glory? This invites us into a response of *humble gratitude*. So that is the first of the implications for lived Christian faith: fostering a sense of gratitude in response to God's love for us.

Second, as we return to the gospel, we see that Jesus's actions were low key, drama free, and a simple response of kindness. But what power was behind that action—changing water into wine. And we know from the gospels that Jesus transformed lives in these gestures of kindness, forgiveness, healing. While I am not reducing the call of the gospel to simply being nicer to one another, there is a reminder here that these gestures of care and compassion are central to how we live the gospel. Revealing the glory of God is done in small ways as well as through changes in structures and preaching the gospel in words. We reveal God's presence and glory in the everyday actions of life, through the *kindness* we express, particularly to those on the margins.

Third, if we look now to the beginning of the gospel story we're reminded that it was Mary who set that work into action. What led her to invite Jesus to take action that day, to respond to the need at hand? Perhaps she recognized a change in him, a new sense of purpose. While Jesus might have protested, "My hour has not yet come," this was not what Mary thought. So Mary models for us a third way in which we reflect the God's presence and glory: by encouraging, inviting, nurturing others to use the gifts they have received, gifts given for the good of all and the glory of God. Through bringing words of encouragement and hope to those whose voices are not yet heard, or to those who think their hour hasn't or won't come, we contribute to an awareness of God's presence in the world. We can reveal God's glory by reminding ourselves and others that the nurturing "moms" in our lives are usually right.

As we move into the second week in Ordinary Time, may we be those who intentionally reflect God's glory through a sense of gratitude, through actions of kindness, and by nurturing within one another the voices that preach the gospel in word and action.

Third Sunday in Ordinary Time

The Spirit as urban pigeon

CARMEN NANKO-FERNÁNDEZ

Nehemiah 8:2–4a, 5–6, 8–10
Psalm 19:8, 9, 10, 15
1 Corinthians 12:12–30
Luke 1:1–4; 4:14–21

Jesus returns to the barrio of his youth and reminds the assembled of what he has learned from the heart of his pueblo. The ancient wisdom he has been raised in is his, and there, in the company of his townspeople, he has come home to demonstrate that he has learned well. He claims for himself the familiar words of the prophet Isaiah, "The Spirit of God is upon me." Anointing by the Spirit, however, comes with responsibilities. Such anointing demands the work of justice: freeing captives, liberating the oppressed, bringing good news to the poor. But Luke's Jesus reminds us—a few verses later—that such work is risky business because "Truly I tell you, no prophet is accepted in their own hometown" (Luke 4:24).

For too long we have domesticated the Holy Spirit, imagining a peaceful white dove as a comforter to support the status quo, or as an advocate without the sharp edge of advocacy. We prefer a Spirit less persistent, less irritating, less demanding than the one that gets Jesus run out of his own hometown. We do not appreciate a dis-comforter who shakes us out of

111

our comfort zones, who finds in our diversity new ways to make common cause. We avoid a Spirit who vexes and cajoles us to be prophetic advocates *en conjunto* (collaboratively) **with** those of us and among us who are pushed to the margins in Church and society, *familia y nación*. The incarnation of the Spirit is not best represented by *una paloma blanca* (a white dove); it is more like the ubiquitous urban pigeon—disruptive, discomforting, irritating.

The incarnation of the Spirit is to be found in prophetic communities rich in diversity and animated by *el espíritu de Dios*. St. Paul admonishes the Corinthians to see themselves in this light, especially when considering their spiritual gifts. His metaphor of the body is both helpful and limited. The call to perceive themselves as an integral whole whose fates and fortunes impact the entire body focuses the Corinthians, and subsequent interpreters, to envision community in terms of interdependence and mutuality. At the same time, Paul's analogy, because of its attention to the so-called "less presentable" and "weaker" parts, unintentionally leads to interpretations that privilege socio-economic power, ableism, maleness, and whiteness.

Scholars and theologians who write from perspectives and experiences within disability studies insist that all bodies are not the same. Human bodies are all different, and not all body parts are necessary for function or quality of life. Experiences of disability shift the focus away from body as if it were an abstraction and toward an emphasis on the lived particularity of embodiedness. Theologian John Swinton proposes, "As we gaze upon our different bodies, rather than assuming that there is a need for healing and change, either now or in the future, we can recognize each one is a site of holiness and a place of meeting."*

---

*John Swinton, "Many Bodies, Many Worlds," in *Disability*, Christian Reflection: A Series in Faith and Ethics (Waco, TX: Baylor University Press, 2012), 18–24.

The incarnation of the Spirit is to be found in prophetic communities, a diversity lived at the intersections of embodied differences. *Somos* (we are) *comunidades* that live on hyphens and *arrobas* (at signs—@s). *Hablamos* (we speak) *español, inglés, espanglish,* numerous sign languages, and even emoji—to name just a few of the many languages in which the Spirit finds expression among us today. *Somos* (We are) *inmigrantes, migrantes,* citizens, alternately documented, and, increasingly, digital natives. *Somos* LGBTQ and straight, and more than a few of us unnecessarily fear each other. We are young and not so young anymore. Some of us move though the day with autism, with wheelchairs, with confidence, or with joys and sorrows guarded in the quiet recesses of our hearts. *Somos curanderas* (healers), caregivers, yet all of us are in need of care.

El Espiritu de Dios that breathes *la vida (the life)* into each one of us, *el Espíritu* that breathes upon us, *el Espíritu* that encourages us to exhale, is the same *Espíritu* that urges us on to cry out *¡basta ya!* (enough already!) to all that stifles its movement for justice *en nuestras comunidades y casas* (in our communities and homes), in our churches, in our countries, *y en nuestro mundo* (in our world).

¡Pa'lante (Onward) *en el Spiritu de Dios!**

---

*Parts of this homily are a revised version of Carmen M. Nanko-Fernández, "¡Una Pneumatología de Basta Ya!," in *Sermons from the Latino/a Pulpit,* ed. Elieser Valentin (Eugene, OR: Wipf and Stock, 2017), 28–34.

Fourth Sunday in Ordinary Time

Love never fails us

FLORA X. TANG

Jeremiah 1:4–5, 17–19
Psalm 71:1–2, 3–4, 5–6, 15–17
1 Corinthians 12:31—13:13
Luke 4:21–30

"Isn't this the son of Joseph?" the people of Nazareth say about Jesus in today's gospel. In this gospel passage, Jesus returns home to Nazareth after performing miracles and preaching God's good news elsewhere. But rather than being welcomed by the people who have known him since he was young, the people of Jesus's hometown refused to take him seriously.

"Isn't this just the son of Joseph?" they ask. "Isn't this just the carpenter boy?"

The people of Nazareth refuse to believe that Jesus has since then grown into someone different, someone with convictions about God's good news that are different from theirs. *Because* Jesus doesn't fit in with their image of what Jesus *should* be like, he is rejected by his home community and driven away.

Now, some suggest that the Gospel of Luke placed this story here to emphasize that Jesus's salvation is not only for the Jewish people, but also for Gentiles and converts. While Luke may be trying to make this point by highlighting throughout his gospel the many ways that Jesus's *own* people have rejected him, we *today* can be reminded that we as Gentiles and Christians are *not* more worthy of God's love than our Jewish siblings—and that interpretations that blame Jewish people for rejecting or killing Jesus easily lead us to the sin of anti-Semitism.

In fact, Jesus's experience of being rejected in today's gospel prompts us to ask ourselves: how often do *we* reject and turn away people in our lives because they no longer fit the image of who we think they are? How often do we *also* make the mistake of looking at our loved ones, and saying something along the lines of, "Isn't this the son of Joseph?" or "Why isn't this person the same as who they had been before?" or "Why has this person changed?"

Whether intentionally or not, we may think or say these things when we look at our children who have grown up to have different convictions, and we lament or become angry at them for being different from how we raised them. We may think these things when we interact with our elderly family members with dementia and they behave in ways that are so different from the way they were when they were healthy. Or, when our friends come out to us as queer or transgender, we might take a while to accept them for who they are. Sometimes, we might end up rejecting people whom we used to love, simply because they are or act differently today.

We see a similar storyline in our first reading from Jeremiah. The prophet Jeremiah also experiences opposition from his own people, perhaps because they *also* did not expect him to become a prophet, or perhaps he defied their expectations a little too much. While *his people* reject him and come after him, God does not leave Jeremiah alone in his rejection, but strengthens him and protects him against his enemies.

Sometimes we might find ourselves in the position of the townspeople of Jesus and Jeremiah. We might find ourselves clinging to the way things used to be, and the way *people* used to be. That's normal, because change is never easy, and we might also be scared of how fast things are changing. In these moments, the gospel today reminds us that it's not just about *our* feelings: it is painful and scary for Jeremiah to experience rejection, as it is painful for Jesus to be forced out of his hometown. In such moments, God is calling us to welcome our friends and family members for the way they are now different, and to listen to what they have to say to us.

Sometimes, we might find ourselves in the position of those who are rejected, of Jesus or Jeremiah in today's readings. We go home to a place we love, but are rejected by our loved ones for who we are today or the things we do. God reminds us that in these moments of rejection, God is on our side, and is proud that we are who we are now. God is proud of us for speaking truth to power, for proclaiming liberation for the oppressed, and for doing the works of mercy. Even when our loved ones and home communities aren't ready to embrace our changes, God is.

At the end of our gospel reading, Jesus passes through the midst of the people and goes away. In walking away, he begins his ministry, finds his new family in his disciples and friends: friends who give him room to proclaim the gospel, friends who do not underestimate him or reject him for who he is. We learn from Jesus's leaving Nazareth that in situations where we are not accepted at all and are experiencing harm, it is okay to set boundaries, walk away, and find new communities of belonging.

So, while we hear in our second reading today from Paul's First Letter to the Corinthians that famous phrase, "Love is patient, and love is kind," we learn from Jeremiah that love is also strong and love is also protective.

We hear from Paul that "love does not seek its own interests, and love is not quick tempered," but we *also* see from today's gospel that love is knowing how to care for yourself, and knowing when to walk away from harm.

We hear that "love does not brood over injury," but we also know that love wants us to seek out joy.

Love "hopes all things and endures all things," but love also calls us to communities and spaces that celebrate us for who we are.

Love looks different in different situations.

Because love never fails us.

Fifth Sunday in Ordinary Time

Turning with God

COLLEEN DULLE

Isaiah 6:1–2a, 3–8
Psalm 138:1–2, 2–3, 4–5, 7–8
1 Corinthians 15:1–11
Luke 5:1–11

Have you ever looked up a timeline of your favorite saint's life—tried to figure out what age they were during the big moments of their life, or figured out how long certain phases of their life lasted? It can reveal some pretty surprising things. For example, twelve years passed from the time St. Ignatius was hit by a cannonball, beginning his conversion, to the time he and the first Jesuits took their vows. Another example: six years passed between Dorothy Day's conversion to Catholicism and her starting the Catholic Worker.

I bring up these examples because they interrupt our usual way of telling these stories. Often, the story of St. Ignatius or Dorothy Day jumps straight from their conversion to the life-defining action that followed it. In reality, that journey often takes years.

This is something that's useful to keep in mind as we hear today's readings about the conversions of Isaiah, Paul, and Simon Peter. In each, the journey from feeling unworthy and unprepared to being called and taking on their mission happens with almost alarming speed! Isaiah says he is "a man of unclean lips," and an angel immediately comes and purifies his lips with an ember. The very next thing he says is in response to God's question, "Whom shall I send?" and he says, "Here I am! Send me!" Likewise, Peter's doubts about Jesus's prediction that he will catch fish are short-lived. He lets this stranger into his boat and does as he says, and immediately, the prediction comes true; Simon's doubt is dispelled. He says, "Depart from me, Lord, for I am a sinful man," but with one (admittedly cryptic) word of reassurance from Jesus—"Do not be afraid, from now on you will be catching men"—Simon, James, and John drop everything to uproot their lives and follow Jesus.

These narratives of one life-changing moment that immediately spurs a person to action can seem highly improbable when we look at our own lives. And, in case we were worried about that being a fault in us, we can see that it's unrealistic for the saints too! But I think these stories do have some important lessons for us about how conversion happens.

The first is this. Concern about how quickly everything happens aside, these readings really highlight *how important those first moments of encountering God are*. For Paul, encountering the risen Jesus on the road to Damascus was shocking. It was the event that defined everything else, that he was still reflecting on years later as he wrote letters to the Christian communities he'd come to know. These readings invite us to look back at our own transformative experiences of encounter with Christ. Maybe you've had a few. Ponder that moment or those moments in your memory. What effect has it had on your life? Are its ripples still visible today? How, this week, can you honor that experience?

Here's the second lesson. As we see with the saints I mentioned, and even with the biblical figures whose conversions seemed so sudden, *those first transformative encounters with God are only ever the beginning* of an ongoing relationship, an ongoing conversion. For Isaiah, it was the beginning of a life of prophecy that would produce some of the most beautiful predictions of the Messiah who was to come. For Paul, that conversion would spark his journey to becoming a leader of a community he once persecuted, and it would lead him to jail. For Peter, the stranger in the boat whom he decided to follow would become one of his closest friends, someone he would lose, and for whom he would ultimately die.

I'm currently writing a biography of the French poet, social worker, and Catholic mystic Madeleine Delbrêl. She is sometimes nicknamed the "French Dorothy Day" because her life followed a similar trajectory, from a free-thinking, Bohemian adolescence to an unexpected conversion to Catholicism, to a life of radical love, living among people whom polite society had cast out: in her case, communist factory workers living outside Paris. Like the other saints I've mentioned, Madeleine is someone who had a definite conversion experience. Late in her life, she was still jotting down the date she identified as the day of her conversion on scraps of paper, to honor it. But it would be ten years between that date and her moving to Ivry, the communist suburb where she ministered. She understood that conversion is an ongoing process. She liked to talk about it as a dance, breaking the word into its Latin roots: "*con-*" or "with," and "*vertere*" or "turn." "To turn with," like dancing with a partner. God guides us in the dance, but as any good dance partner knows, following isn't passive: You have to be super-present, attentive, free to move where your partner leads, but also sure enough in your abilities and your partner's to take those steps decisively and confidently.

That brings me to my third point. Each of the conversion stories we heard today were preceded by doubt and a sense of unworthiness. Isaiah has "unclean lips"; Paul writes that he was the last one to see Christ; Simon Peter tells Jesus, "Depart from me, Lord, for I am a sinful man." Each of these people, all towering figures in salvation history, need a word of encouragement to overcome their hesitancy and begin their work. So here's a last question to reflect on: If we are to be Christ to one another, *what can we do to encourage and empower* the prophets of our day to speak, or the saints of our day to minister?

Sixth Sunday in Ordinary Time

Love demands doing something with our feet

BRIDGET BEARSS, RSCJ

Jeremiah 17:5–8
Psalm 1:1–2, 3, 4, and 6
1 Corinthians 15:12, 16–20
Luke 6:17, 20–26

We are called today—

to be people of the heart, to be those for whom love takes form, not in the Valentine form, but in the real stuff of life.

I am a Religious of the Sacred Heart, an international congregation of women for whom our charism animates both our identity and mission "to discover and reveal God's love."

We are drawn to the heart of Jesus, the heart of God—where the heart of humanity is united in the paschal mystery of both suffering and incarnation . . . where all is one.

It is from that heart, opened by love and my mission as an educator with a passion for justice, and the spirit

of an artist who is really a story-teller, that I am here
to break open the scripture with you.

My parents were married for sixty-six years—sixty-six
real years of the tough stuff of life—from my father's years
in the Navy, to raising five kids in tough economic times, to
the losses and re-imagining that happens with dreams lost
and found—and with seventeen geographic moves along
life's journey. It was the real stuff of life, what love that requires a faith that depends on hope in something unseen
looks like.

After my mother died, my father was lost. He had planned
to go first. A diabetic, every night at 10 o'clock he and my
mother shared a snack that helped regulate his blood sugar
through the night. Every night at 10 o'clock, they broke
bread—literally: they ate toast.

I was with my father a couple of weeks after my mother
died, and one night at 10 o'clock I said to him, "I'll go and
make us some toast." He shook his head with definitive clarity—"No. No toast." Presuming this was to protect his open
heart of grief, I said, "Because you ate toast with Mom every
night?"

"No," he said, "Because I hate toast." I was baffled and
sat back down.

"Wait. For sixty-six years, every night you ate toast and
you don't like toast?"

"That's right," he replied.

"Why didn't you ever say something?" I asked.

"Because your mother loved toast. That's why I ate
toast."

That's what it means, for me, to dwell in the heart of
God. It is not soft or luxurious. It is to be so willing to step
outside the ego, the self, that we are drawn into the heart
of another. We are drawn into the heart of God. . . . Sometimes we are the one who makes the toast for another and

sometimes we are the one who eats it because that's what love calls us to do. It is never one or the other—it is always both/and.

We live in a divided world, and we are the instruments of the heart of God who choose to build bridges of relationship in places, structures, attitudes, and experiences of difference. We do not remain in the polarity but live from the unity of knowing that we—each one of us—has the possibility to be a prophet or a persecutor.

Today's readings might seem to create an image of dualism, of polarity, which reflects the culture in which we live. We are presented with "the in" and "the out"—Jeremiah's portrayal of the barren and of the fertile, the distinction of which Paul speaks between believers in resurrection and the unenlightened, the contrast made by the psalmist between the way of the wicked and the way of the one planted near running streams. It is not hard to know where we would want to be.

And yet, as I approach twenty-five years of being present at twelve-step recovery meetings, I stand on a stretch of level ground with Luke, listening to the words of Jesus, and I know that my journey has been one in which I have been on both the side of the "Blessed Builders" and the side of the "Woe Warned."

I have been among the persecuted and the prophetic. I have stood as one who has judged those I have determined unworthy and one who has been judged and is in need of compassion and forgiveness in the experience of being human. I have stood in the midst of those whose commitment to Catholic social teaching leads to active protest and public witness, and I have seen compassion and right action from those to whom I stand in opposition and judge as in need of "woe-warning."

Each of us, I believe, at some moment in our lives, can find ourselves among the wheat and among chaff. At some moments, we feel like a barren bush in the desert and at other times like a tree planted beside the waters of a stream. There are moments in each of our lives when hope in the God of yield and plenty has felt distant and others when we rejoice in living lives that proclaim resurrection. Many of us, I suspect—if not all of us—find ourselves sometimes as "bringers of blessings" and at other times as hearers of "warnings of woe."

Today, we are issued both an invitation and a choice. God leaves us free to look within our hearts and see what love calls us to do—AND where our feet need to take us. Do we nourish the soil in which we are planted by keeping our eyes open, our hearts wide, and our hands outstretched? Our past history, our giving record, the social action we took yesterday do not exempt us from opening our hearts so that our insides and our outsides match today. We are challenged again, in this day, to make of our lives a gospel to be read by others, to make visible the vision of Jesus and the tools he left us.

When our eyes are open to the needs of the person next to us, when we can see the inequality promulgated by our silence, then we know that the dream of God (the Reign of God) in our midst requires something of us today. Where will our feet take us? Love demands doing something with our feet.

In our midst is the invitation—the call—to make room at the table for both the Blessed Bringers and the Woe-Warned, where each of us makes room for the other, I for you and you for me, so that regardless of the category in which we place one another, we can hope again that the dream of God is our dream. . . .

A dream where we will each have the chance to make the toast and to share the bread of love.

To be the bread of life with and for one another.

What does love ask of us this day?

Seventh Sunday in Ordinary Time

What you can do with a water jug and a spear

DEBORAH WILHELM

1 Samuel 26:2, 7–9, 12–13, 22–23
Psalm 103:1–2, 3–4, 8, 10, 12–13
1 Corinthians 15:45–49
Luke 6:27–38

Imagine for a moment that you are King Saul, and that you (and all of your troops) are deeply, deliciously asleep. Actually, probably half of you right now are thinking, *Oh yeah, I'd love some deep, delicious sleep*, and the other half are probably thinking, *I'd love it if my children or students or colleagues would fall into a deep delicious sleep!*

Ah . . . but back to Saul—or you, as Saul. You've placed your spear and your water jug carefully beside you. Off to dreamland.

But what you don't know is that also beside you stand two wide-awake people, one of whom wants to pin you to the ground with your own spear, and the other one of whom has the power to say, "Do it." You'll never know what hit you.

In our first reading today, Abishai is ready to kill Saul, but David says that it would be wrong to harm the Lord's anointed. I get the struggle. Tensions in Israel are high, lives are on the line, the country is at stake, the leadership and future are uncertain. Wait . . . am I talking about Israel, or about us? And look: everyone's asleep, and there's a spear, just begging to be picked up. It seems to me right now, especially during these contentious and chaotic times, that we're all somewhat ready to pick up a spear and pin our enemies to the ground. Today's version of a spear might be something obvious, like a gun or a bomb. Or today's spear might be more subtle, like a piece of legislation. Today's spear might even be an anonymous letter. An angry word. A trashcan full of single-use plastic containers, not-yet-spoiled food, and clothes that we're just tired of, all headed for the dump.

It's understandable to want to be Abishai. And easy to pick up the spear. But we can also be David. The pause for that conversation between them is a gift; it takes place only because everyone's asleep—and as the text says, that deep sleep is the work of the Lord. Their conversation is in that liminal space, neither here nor there, in which decisions are made and carried out, and lives are changed. Because at some point in our lives, we're all going to be Saul—broken, vulnerable, and nevertheless anointed by God. In fact, we are Saul already: Saul's water jug reminds me that each of us at baptism is anointed by the Holy Spirit into Christ's anointing as priest, prophet, and king. David takes both spear and water jug as a sign, and then, later, he returns them. We, too, are gifted with God's mercy, beloved of the Creator, and called to lives of mercy and love, water jug in hand.

Eighth Sunday in Ordinary Time

The tree known by her fruit

JENNIFER THEBY-QUINN

Sirach 27:4–7
Psalm 92:2–3, 13–14, 15–16
1 Corinthians 15:54–58
Luke 6:39–45

A few years ago, I had the opportunity to play a really hilarious role in a very silly play by Mark Twain. My character dressed herself like a toy doll from the mid-nineteenth century. I wore a satin and lace dress, an impossibly large wig, and obnoxiously long false eyelashes. One day, while I was onstage, one of my lashes popped halfway off my lid. It sort of drooped into my field of vision, blurring everything in the footlights. It wasn't painful but it made the set—a French-style drawing room with all manner of stools and settees and poufs that created a kind of obstacle course—that much more difficult to navigate, and by the end of the scene my eyes were watering to the point where my cast mate had to guide me offstage. Just the other day, backstage in a different production, I applied my mascara perhaps too quickly, and poked myself in the eye with the mascara wand. My eye watered and turned red and I had to carry a tissue backstage with me to blot it before heading on. Just this morning, I put my glasses on and realized right away that it had been some time since I'd last cleaned them. It was like trying to read emails through wax paper.

As a person who is blessed with the gift of relatively good sight, I notice when I can't see something, and it drives me bonkers when I get something in my eyes. It's uncomfortable to be without this sense; it can be painful, for sure, but mostly I feel vulnerable.

In today's gospel, Jesus describes what to me sounds like a horrendous obstruction. I don't like splinters anywhere, but a splinter in your eye sounds awful. And that's not even the one applied to us readers! Jesus says, "Why do you notice the splinter in your sister or brother's eye, but you do not perceive the wooden beam in your own?" I can barely handle a speck of dust in my eyes when the wind kicks up; how do you think I'd handle a two-by-four?

We know what Jesus is getting at, because to take him literally would be absurd. Anyone who has ever flown on an airplane knows you secure the oxygen mask on your face before you take care of your kid's oxygen mask, because if you pass out before you can manage it, you've just made matters worse. Same thing here: it is OBVIOUS that if you literally cannot see because you have a tree sticking out of your eye, there's no way you'll be able to help someone with a tiny shard in theirs. It would be ridiculous to behave that way, and no one *wants* to be ridiculous.

But we know, we know that Jesus doesn't mean our literal eyes. Luke uses the Greek word "ὀφθαλμῷ (ophthalmō)" which does literally mean eye, but also means vision, the mind's eye, a person's mode of perceiving, understanding the world around her.

And Jesus asks: Why, why is it that you are so quick to perceive in your mind's eye the flaws and failures of others—the things that cloud their vision: their pettiness, their pride, their politics—when you so thoroughly fail to see what is yours to change? Would you not do better to fix your own perception?

My own pride is so great a thing that it can indeed blind me. Convinced as I so often am of my own rightness, my own perception of what is true, of what ought to be done, I am like a horse with blinders on: I cannot always see what is happening to my left or right. I am forever praying for the humility to recognize when I am stuck in a pattern of self-certainty.

I suspect that one of the major sins of our age is a failure of imagination: to be incapable of dreaming that we might not have the answer, and that the truth may, in fact, lie inside a perspective we've yet to consider. It's a failure to pursue humility. A failure to approach the troubles of our time with anything other than an angular, edged, iron fist of self-righteousness.

Sandwiched as this gospel reading is between the great Love Commandment to "love our enemies and do good to those who hate us" (v. 27) and the image of a house built on a strong foundation as opposed to a shaky one, we can begin to draw out the following conclusion: loving my neighbors— my colleagues, the students I minister to, my relatives whose perspectives just have me shaking my head—LOVING them has almost nothing to do with judging them or trying to "fix" them, but it most certainly has to do with looking to myself, considering what needs remedying in my own mindset, my own pride, my own pettiness, my own politics. With our attention focused here, we discover, as the psalmist says:

> *The just shall flourish like the palm tree, shall grow like*
> *   a cedar of Lebanon.*
> *Planted in the house of the LORD,*
> *they shall flourish in the courts of our God. They shall*
> *   bear fruit even in old age,*
> *they will stay fresh and green....* (Ps 92:13–15)

That's what the firm foundation looks like: a tree, with roots reaching deep to her Source, who stays near the water that gives her life, a person unafraid of vulnerability, unafraid of being wrong, because she is deeply, deeply rooted in the radical and boundless love of Jesus. This is the tree Jesus mentions at the end of today's reading: the tree known by her fruit. I'd so much rather be a healthy fruit tree than a two-by-four.

Thirteenth Sunday in Ordinary Time

The beauty of the invitation

ELIZABETH TURNWALD

1 Kings 19:16b, 19–21
Psalm 16:1–2, 5, 7–8, 9–10, 11
Galatians 5:1, 13–18
Luke 9:51–62

Around this time two years ago I was wandering the streets of Assisi and Rome while on a pilgrimage with a group of students from my school. The point of the journey was to take in the beauty around us and to apply it to the process of discernment—to see how gratitude and presence can lead us closer to the Divine. As this was the summer before my senior year, I felt a weighty ultimatum as though I would need to have my entire future mapped out before graduation. I had been praying for about a year beforehand that on this pilgrimage I might receive some sign or grace that would lead me closer to my vocation; and it happened. I experienced such a grace within the first two days of this journey—specifically in seeing a vision of myself entering a ministerial setting, working with women, and studying theology and women's studies in graduate school. I was filled with a deep sense of peace and gratitude . . . for about thirty-six hours. Then, for the next nine days of the pilgrimage, I spiraled. I dug through all of the ways it wouldn't work, all of the reasons I shouldn't do it. And then I spent the rest of that summer and into the fall twisting it in my hands until it hung limp and lifeless, stowed away without air or light in the obscure corners of my mind. Instead of letting it unfold, I constructed walls around it. I questioned, "Well, how would that work?" and "What would my timeline look like?" and "Oh my goodness, what would so-and-so think of that?"

We spend so much time as Christians telling ourselves (and too often *others*) how we surrender to the will of God, how Jesus is all we need, how we place all of our trust in him. But when it comes down to the wire, do we? In the gospel this week, Jesus calls the disciples to put their money where their mouths are. Various disciples approach him saying, "I will follow you wherever you go, Lord." And Jesus answers them, "Foxes have dens, and birds of the sky have nests, but the Son of Man has nowhere to rest his head." Is this a warning to us? Is he lamenting how impractical and idealistic his followers are? Is he somewhat patronizingly remarking, "Aw, that's cute." They think it's as easy as speaking their loyalty into existence—as though stating, "I will be faithful," implies a lifetime without questioning, doubt, or fear.

When Jesus finally invites one of the disciples explicitly, saying, "Follow me," the disciple replies, "Lord, let me go first to bury my father." Jesus replies, "Let the dead bury their dead. But you, go and proclaim the kingdom of God." It sounds surprisingly harsh at first, as though Jesus is heartlessly forbidding him to grieve with his family. But rather than interpret this as some political, anti-family rhetoric, it feels like Jesus is challenging his disciples' will and their perceptions of what it means to surrender. They're quite literally following him around in the desert, much like on a pilgrimage, believing themselves to be ready and open to the movement of the Spirit in their lives. However, the second Jesus verbalizes his desire for them to become co-ministers with him, the disciples automatically push back and say, "Okay, but first . . . ," putting their own priorities and timelines and desires ahead of a Divine invitation.

This struggle to fully surrender to the will of God is a common theme of the readings and gospel this week, and of my own journey as well. In the competitive, capitalist U.S. society in which I was raised, "surrender" often has a connotation of giving up, of quitting and throwing in the towel because the fight isn't worth the energy. But in the Christian tradition, it's quite the opposite. It means letting go and giving in because we are so fully invested in hearing what the Creator has in store for us. Instead of fighting against the tide of this Divine movement within us, we are called to follow, to answer not with "Okay, but first . . . ," but rather with gratitude and restfulness.

This is something that I personally grapple with, and I think I can safely bet that most people do too. We can get so caught up in the preparation that we don't appreciate the invitation. But the marvelous thing about God, this all-forgiving, all-patient Universal Love, is that even when we don't answer "correctly," she finds a way of repeating herself; and she will continue asking until we're ready. It's a cycle, a pattern, and a living relationship. We won't always get it right the first time, but we will eventually discover that sweet bliss of open surrender. We simply must continue witnessing, embracing, and resting in the beauty of the invitation so that when we hear it we can answer with a grateful and resolute "Thank you. Yes."

Fourteenth Sunday in Ordinary Time

The consolation of God, our Mother

EMILY RAUER DAVIS

Isaiah 66:10–14c
Psalm 66:1–3, 4–5, 6–7, 16, 20
Galatians 6:14–18
Luke 10:1–12, 17–20

When my children were infants and toddlers, there was nothing more heartbreaking—or heartwarming—than pulling them into my arms to comfort them when they were hurt or distressed. Whatever the injury—a skinned knee, a bruised ego, illness, or disappointment—a hug and some soothing words usually seemed to take the edge off the pain. I remember feeling the same way when I was a child and needed comfort. There was something about the feel of my mom's strong arms and the softness of her cheek, the smell of her skin and the sound of her voice that put me at ease and made me feel as though everything would be okay. My mom offered the solace I needed to head back out into whatever I was doing, confident in her love for me and reassured of my place in the world.

This is why today's first reading resonates so powerfully with me: "As nurslings, you shall be carried in her arms, and fondled in her lap; as a mother comforts her child, so will I comfort you." The image of God as mother is one that I can relate to both as a child being held and consoled and as a mother offering solace. Although I will never be able to fully grasp the depth and breadth of God's immense love for us, I think the closest I will ever come is through the maternal love I've both received and given.

The gospel reading, on the other hand, has a bit of a different tone. When Jesus missions the seventy-two to go out and share the Good News, he tells them to expect difficulty and pain: "I am sending you like lambs among wolves," he warns. Their instructions are to stick together, live simply, graciously accept hospitality, and shake off any ill-will. We don't get much detail about their adventures, but we can presume that they achieved at least a modicum of success, as they come back "rejoicing" after having cast out demons in the name of Jesus.

Our readings today are rich with spiritual wisdom as we consider the current state of our world. The Earth suffers under the weight of climate change, pollution, and deforestation. As a people, we are increasingly divided and demoralized. Racism, homophobia, sexism, ableism, classism, and xenophobia are as prevalent as ever. And the institutions we've come to depend on out of necessity or tradition or choice— including our government and the Church—have become repositories for disillusionment and, often, disgust. How are we to proceed as disciples of Christ who are called to be conduits of God's love and mercy in the world? On the surface, the picture looks bleak, unforgiving, perhaps even hopeless. Lambs among wolves, indeed.

Yet the word that echoes through nearly all of our readings today is "rejoice" ("...your heart shall rejoice," "...let us rejoice in God," "...the seventy-two returned rejoicing"). In spite of the hardships we face, or creeping feelings of despair, we are invited to recall the love of God as Mother: nurturing us, consoling us, and reassuring us of our place in the world. We are called to be a people of hope as we go about our work as disciples in our broken world, with God's promise of abundant, gratuitous love as our foundation.

Remembering this is not always easy; it's certainly something I've struggled with in my own ministry. I've sat with students coming to terms with the sins of the only Church they've ever belonged to, questioning whether or not they want to stay and often wondering where God is in the mess. I've commiserated with colleagues and friends as we search for new and creative ways to raise our voices in protest of injustices both sacred and secular. It feels increasingly difficult to explain to others, and sometimes even to myself, why I continue to do this work in this Church.

And yet the image of God as Mother offers something in addition to tenderness and compassion. It offers the hope that something new can and will be born into the world: a "new creation," as Paul writes in his letter to the Galatians. The definitive manifestation of this newness, for Christians, is Christ himself. He who ate with the outcast, touched the untouchable, and loved the despised and forgotten was put to death and then came back in a way that was wholly new and mysterious... unlike anything that had come before. A new creation, rooted in peace and mercy and love, is what we are promised. It is the reality for which we are told to rejoice. And not, as Jesus reminds the seventy-two in today's gospel, for what we can *do*, but for who we *are*: God's beloved, whose names are written in heaven.

So I rejoice in those beloved whose presence brings color, laughter, and consolation to my world, whose names are written in my own book of days:

I rejoice in my colleagues in ministry, companions on the journey whose faith and generosity fortify my own....

I rejoice in my students, whose compassion and idealism fill me with hope. . . .

I rejoice in the love of family and friends, my community of saints, my cheerleaders and challengers. . . .

I rejoice in my children, who remind me to see the world through eyes of imagination and wonder. . . .

And I rejoice in God as Mother, whose love is always there for the taking, arms open wide to receive and comfort and then send us back out, together, to do her work in the world.

Fifteenth Sunday in Ordinary Time

Is neighbor a noun or a verb?

ANN GARRIDO

Deuteronomy 30:10–14
Psalm 69:14, 17, 30–31, 33–34, 36, 37
Colossians 1:15–20
Luke 10:25–37

Picture this: you wake to find yourself in a strange bed in a strange room, unable to move your right arm and tasting blood on your split lip. Your right eye is swollen shut, and you can only partially open your puffy left eye. But this takes so much effort that you close it again, sliding back into darkness.

When you wake anew, you see sunlight streaming through the crack beneath the door, illuminating beside you a bedside table with a cup of tea. Where are you?

To deepen the mystery, the door swings open to reveal the silhouette of a woman you don't recognize. "I was wondering when you would wake up," she says. "How is your head feeling?"

"What happened?" you ask.

"You were beat up...we think by robbers hiding in the thicket beside the road."

"Who brought me here?"

"A neighbor."

"But who? What was their name?"

She shrugs. "He had to go on, but said that he'd check back in on you and settle your tab."

You sigh. Ahhh, a neighbor. What a relief. But how could that be? You are far from home. Who would *you* know also traveling on that road? What are the chances a neighbor would pass by? You rack your brain as to who it could be. People only have a small number of neighbors in the world.

You've heard somewhere in life about the work of the British evolutionary psychologist Robin Dunbar. It was in some newspaper or science journal you picked up somewhere. About how there is a correlation between the size of a primate's brain and the size of a primate's social network. Inside that network—or tribe, one might say—the monkey or ape will watch out for its fellow monkeys or apes, demonstrating benevolence and cooperation. But outside that tribe, the primate will not. Indeed, it'll see members even of its own species as threats.

Dunbar thinks that based on the size of the human brain, our social networks would naturally average around 150 people. And he has a lot of examples from human history to back that number up: the size of hunter-gatherer communities tends to around 150. The ancient remains of Neolithic villages in the Middle East—around 150. The size of a military unit during the Roman Empire. The Domesday Book recording the population of towns in medieval England. Even the Christmas card list of the modern British family. All suggest that humans have tended to cluster in groups of about 150 people.

So, for someone to have stopped and become so personally involved in your situation, it must have been someone within your "150." But *who* could it have been? You are running through lists of possibilities in your mind when there is a rattling noise outside and a car with a tail pipe in need of repair pulls loudly into the parking lot. The woman moves to open the blinds and you turn to look out the window. You spot an old jalopy plastered with bumper stickers from the last election that make you cringe.

"Oh, here he is now," she says.

"Who?" you reply.

"The guy who brought you here. Carried you from the back seat of his vehicle."

He steps out of the car, but you have no idea who this is. Do you have amnesia as well?

"That is not one of my neighbors," you say.

"Really?" the woman who runs the inn asks. "Hmm. Is neighbor a noun or a verb? Is it someone you live near... or someone who draws near when you need them? Is a neighbor something you have or something you do?"

Everything about this man makes your hair stand on end. Listen as he greets the receptionist outside in the hall. By the way he talks, you can tell there is no way he is from back home. The innkeeper turns to you and says, "I imagine you'll want to speak with him."

Your head begins to ache in a different sort of way. Yes. But maybe no. He looks, he thinks, he speaks so differently from you. What if he is looking for money? For a favor in return? You owe him everything. How can you possibly repay that? How do you feel about your savior being a Samaritan? How is this even possible? Robin Dunbar would say that all of human history—indeed all of evolution—is not set up for this kind of thing to happen!

"I'll leave so that the two of you can talk," the innkeeper says.

And I, your narrator, will take that cue to leave you also, so that in your reflection on the scripture of this Sunday, you may continue the conversation. Think carefully about what you want to say, if anything, to your Good Samaritan... and what you want to ask. Who is he? Why did he stop? And why did he become so personally invested in your mishap?

Evolutionarily speaking, care and cooperation are not set up to happen outside one's social network, and yet.... What might he have to say that Robin Dunbar would never have to say about what it means to be a neighbor?

Sixteenth Sunday in Ordinary Time

The truth about Martha and Mary

SUSAN FLEMING MCGURGAN

Genesis 18:1–10a
Psalm 15:2–3, 3–4, 5
Colossians 1:24–28
Luke 10:38–42

As so often happens with scripture, we tend to glide over the surface of this strange little story, smoothing out the rough corners, spackling over the cracks, and taping together the jagged edges that don't quite meet—believing that because it is familiar and known we have it all figured out. But all the spackle in the hardware store can't hide the fact that this is still a strange little story.

On the surface, Martha, the older sister, is busy with many things—distracted, flustered, on edge from welcoming Jesus and his disciples into her home, perhaps more than a bit jealous of Mary, who leaves her with the dishes and the dust bunnies while she sits at the feet of the Master.

"Martha" has sometimes become a byword for someone who's, well, a little too busy for her own good. Someone who's busy and never lets you forget it. Someone who volunteers to take on more and more, and then wants to volunteer YOU, too. As one preacher said, Martha is a woman who "interrupted Jesus to talk about chores." For some, a Martha is the quintessential martyr; a woman whose good works are dished up with a side of commentary and a pinch of complaint. Teachings on this passage often focus on the tension between two approaches to discipleship, such as: *Living a Mary Life in a Martha World, The Practical Life of Service vs. the Spiritual Life of Contemplation, To Do or to Be.* Or, discussions play into subtle and sometimes not so subtle stereotypes and tropes about feminine jealousy, womanly meddling, girlish dysfunction: *The Jealous Sister, Competition among Church Ladies, The Right Attitude for Women's Service.* Often, exegesis of this passage proposes the rather obvious insight that we are called to be both Martha and Mary. We are called to integrate: Listening *and* Doing; Action *and* Contemplation; Dwelling in the Word *and* Living Out the Word. And the trick is to find balance between the busy Martha and contemplative Mary who live within each of us. Martha and Mary are even seen as models for the pilgrim and heavenly Church—the Church Militant and the Church Triumphant. On earth, we live as Martha, the pilgrim church, but we strive for the heavenly Church to come, as typified by Mary.

There is nothing wrong with these interpretations, except for the blatantly condescending ones, and much to be said for those that point out the need to balance the tension between action and reflection, doing and being. But scripture is seldom so easy, so pat, so one-dimensional. Stories in scripture often need to be turned sideways or even upside down to make sense, and even the simplest and most straightforward teachings of Jesus are rich and complex, filled with invitation, challenge, and surprise.

This particular story has many textual variants. There are verbs that may be translated more than one way that can completely change the meaning; there are disconnects that are not easy to explain away. Why are Martha's actions unsatisfactory?

In his own ministry, Jesus emphasizes feeding people, providing wine and bread and fish; dining, sharing, offering radical hospitality to the point where he and his disciples are criticized for it. *Why is Martha criticized for doing what Jesus himself did?*

Even the interpretation that we should strive for balance between contemplation and action is puzzling, since in this passage, these options are seen as mutually exclusive, diametrically opposed, with one option being approved and the other rejected.

Sorry, Martha, Mary has chosen the better path.

Is this, as many say, a cautionary tale about the spiritual danger of busy-ness severed from prayer, reflection, and study? Or is it not really about Martha at all, but an affirmation of women's discipleship and study, a formal blessing for women like Mary—like us—who choose to "sit at the Master's feet" beside the men? If so, then why the dialogue with Martha?

Is this the narration of an event in the life of Jesus, presented as it happened, or is it, as scripture scholars Elisabeth Schüssler Fiorenza and Barbara Reid suggest, an incident that has been filtered, shifted, re-imagined, and shared through the lens of Luke's early Christian community, a community that may have been struggling to discern and define and re-define women's roles in leadership, study, and *diakonia*—service?*

The text itself does not explicitly refer to a meal, and it does not place Martha in the kitchen or behind a broom— that is our own story, our own image, our own assumption. The text, in fact, uses the word "*diakonia*" for Martha's work; it is a word Luke uses eight times. *Diakoneo* can mean waiting upon, helping to support, doing the work, serving, prepara-

---

*Barbara E. Reid, "Pitting Mary against Martha," in *Choosing the Better Part? Women in the Gospel of Luke* (Collegeville, MN: Liturgical Press, 1996), 144–62.

tion, it can mean many things—and, among them, ministry in the name of the Church.

Is it possible that Martha's distress does not originate in cooking, cleaning, or being relegated to the kitchen, but in something deeper?

Martha's state is typically translated as "distracted, over-burdened, busy," but the verb also commonly means, "to be pulled or dragged away." Does Martha's frustration emerge from pain over a "pulling away" or "taking away" of her place and role in ministry? Could this story reflect a post-Resurrection struggle in the evangelist's community over the proper ministerial roles for women—active or docile? Leader or passive listener?

Is this passage a remnant? A lingering memory from a community that tamed the diaconal ministry of women while advocating for a more traditional feminine role?

Is Martha a cautionary tale for the overwhelmed? Or do we hear in her the anguished voice of a woman who sees her role and her ministerial responsibilities being pulled away, diminished, dismissed, and calling on her sister in ministry to come to her support?

And Mary...

Is Mary the model of a bold disciple, claiming her space among the men, or is she a figure that illustrates the importance of women keeping silence?

I don't know.

And neither do any of the brilliant scholars who study this story.

All we can do is view Mary and Martha and Jesus through the eyes of faith and the crucible of our experience and reflect on the possibilities—knowing and trusting that Christ is with us in the reflection.

We can embrace and emulate the sisters' close relationship with Jesus, a friendship so deep that they trust him with their anger, their silence, their choices. We know that, later, they would trust him even unto death, as he commanded their beloved Lazarus to exit the tomb. We can give thanks for their courage in following Jesus. We know that Martha and Mary, like other women we meet in scripture, lived lives of boldness, whatever else the world may say about them.

They sat at his feet, like Mary.

They served, like Martha.

They said "Yes," like our Lady.

They argued for inclusion, like the Syrophoenician woman. They brought their friends to encounter Jesus, like the woman at the well.

They offered financial support for mission, like Johanna. They led house churches, like Phoebe.

They evangelized, like Priscilla.

They sang of justice, walked in faith, and dreamed of a new and transformed world, enlightened by the light of Christ.

What is the truth about Martha and Mary?

For me, it is enough to know that their faithfulness, their commitment to love and serve, and yes, lead, is our inheritance—yours and mine, passed down from mother to daughter, between sister and sister, disciple to disciple, from woman of faith to woman of faith throughout the ages—whatever our station, whatever our circumstance, whatever our struggles, whatever our personal response to God's call.

Martha is honored as the patron saint of servants, cooks, housewives, butlers, housemaids, laundry workers, hotelkeepers—and that is no surprise. But if you study medieval paintings of Martha, paintings from France, and Italy, and Germany from the fourteenth to sixteenth centuries, you will see something else, altogether—something unexpected. Something bold. Something that invites us to continue to turn our vision of Martha upside down and sideways.

These artists portray Martha as a dragon slayer—a feminine version of St. George. After the Resurrection, legend tells us that Martha subdued a wild creature terrorizing the countryside—conquering it with a cross, some holy water, and her own fierce and unflagging courage.

Martha and Mary: sisters in faith. Homemaker. Student. Disciples. Slayer of Dragons. Choosing Faith. Choosing Jesus. Choosing the better part.

Seventeenth Sunday in Ordinary Time

What trees can teach us about the Lord's Prayer

BRENNA DAVIS

Genesis 18:20–32
Psalm 138:1–2, 2–3, 6–7, 7–8
Colossians 2:12–14
Luke 11:1–13

"A tree gives glory to God by being a tree." This is one of my favorite quotes from Thomas Merton, and I think trees are good models of the dynamics that we find in the Lord's Prayer which we hear in the gospel today. I recently read a book by Leonardo Boff called *The Lord's Prayer: A Prayer of Integral Liberation,* and in it he talks about the multi-directional nature of the Lord's Prayer. If you look at the first half of the prayer, this is really where we focus on God and God's plans and desires for the world in which we live.

As a woman in the Church, I often struggle with male imagery for God and have for a long time, but what I appreciated about Boff's book was that he talked about the idea that this name that Jesus gives God is really a nickname and a term of endearment for a beloved ancestor. And so, as I think in my own life about an ancestor with a nickname, I think of my Gram. She was a kind woman, and every night as

I would fall asleep when I was growing up she would rub my back and just listen to me as I shared concerns about my family or what was happening in the world. So, as we think about the beginning of this prayer and this God that we love, we know that this is a God who loves us and knows us intimately and just wants to rub our backs as we as live our lives and work for justice in the world.

As we move on in the prayer to think about the line "thy will be done," this is really a statement of hope, faith, and trust in God, the belief that God desires a world of peace and justice where all needs are met and everyone can flourish. And so, by speaking this line, we are stating, "I believe in this vision of God's will for the Earth" and want to bring it to fruition.

As we move on to the second half of the prayer, the secondary dynamic, this dynamic is really about being rooted where we are on the holy ground, where we stand as members of a community. We are finite humans with concrete needs. In thinking about "our daily bread," what I find especially beautiful are the plural pronouns that we use throughout the prayer. We remember and affirm that we are a community and that we are interconnected and called to support and love one another.

I recently saw a statistic that said maybe 7 percent of the world's grain comes from Ukraine. When we think about the suffering and war happening there and in other places, this image of grain and of bread is a true reminder that we are intimately interconnected through our food systems in ways that we might not even imagine. And this thought brings us back to trees.

Historically, there's been a way of thinking that forests are areas where trees are fighting each other for resources, "survival of the fittest," but newer science tells us that actually forests are places of collaboration and community. Tree roots interconnect underneath the ground. The mycelium and fungi that grow on these roots allow trees of different species to communicate with each other and share resources between them. If one tree is suffering in one part of the year or doesn't have access to the resources that it needs, another tree can send them along. And it works both ways. The trees are able to meet each other's needs out of their abundance. This is a beautiful image of the way in which we too are called to live as members of the community of God and as people who are trying to bring about God's reign on the earth.

The final dynamic of the last part of the Lord's Prayer is expressed in the phrase "lead us not into temptation." I know that as I do ecology work at the Ignatian Solidarity Network, I think my personal temptation is a temptation to despair, a temptation to hear the news about climate change, or about racial injustice, or about migration justice, and to feel like there's nothing that we can do. It's too late. Hope is lost.

And so, in this way again, the Lord's Prayer is a reminder (and a statement of belief) that, first of all, this work is not mine to do alone. We do it in community. And second, it is a reminder that this God who knows and loves me, and all of us, and who is close enough to rub my back and accompany me, has a great plan for the Earth if I am willing to trust it and do my part to make it a reality.

The final part of today's gospel, when Jesus says, "Ask and you will receive; seek and you will find," really resonates with me. I know that sometimes I get so overwhelmed that I forget to ask. I forget to ask for the help of my neighbor. I forget to ask for the spiritual food that I need from God, for Eucharist. Jesus reminds us that we do not walk alone and that we do this work in community.

Going back to the image of a tree and this multi-directional dynamic, I think that a tree is the image of being deeply rooted in your place and community and in sharing resources and caring for those around us. At the same time its branches are reaching up to the transcendent, to this God who loves us, and who invites us to engage in bringing about the reign of God.

And so my prayer for all of us is that as we enter into the dynamics of the Lord's Prayer, that we can be consoled, that we can trust in God's plan, and that we can be bread for one another and lean on our neighbors when we need the sustenance to carry us forward to bring about the reign of God.

Eighteenth Sunday in Ordinary Time

The riches that truly matter

ELIZABETH GARLOW

Ecclesiastes 1:2; 2:21–23
Psalm 90:3–4, 5–6, 12–13, 14, 17
Colossians 3:1–5, 9–11
Luke 12:13–21

This morning I watched my one-year-old waddle down the sidewalk in her mismatched outfit . . . a sign of the haste of the morning amidst the responsibilities of day-to-day living.

But as I watched her, I couldn't help but reflect on how she was not at all aware or bothered by her poorly coordinated Easter onesie and pair of hot pink shorts on this warm July day in Michigan. . . . In her pure innocence, she has not been captured by a sense of self-consciousness around the signals of prosperity we tend to express in our choices of clothing, personal appearance, housing.

It is so easy for us to be caught up in those status markers sustained by personal wealth. While watching my daughter I admittedly felt a little self-conscious of my rickety car approaching 200,000 miles or the fact that we live in one of the smaller houses on the block.

For many of us, a fixation on material surplus and accumulation gradually creeps into our lives in small but continual ways.

In today's gospel reading, Jesus tells the crowd a parable about a rich man whose land has produced a bountiful harvest. Rather than share that bounty with others, the man decides to build larger barns to store it all and save it for himself, so that he may rest, eat, drink, and be merry for years to come. Jesus tells the crowd to "guard against all greed, for though one may be rich, one's life does not consist of possessions."

Taking Jesus's message to heart will require a profound shift. In fact, today's dominant economic system and the culture it upholds encourage accumulation of wealth and material goods. The mainstreamed and marketized narrative of a good life, characterized by constant expansion and luxury, runs deep in our culture.

Some have noted that we have moved our focus from "the good life" to a fixation on "the goods life." And, in fact, we now live in a society with little to no limits on those goods.

But thankfully many are waking up to the ways that this focus on short-term wealth accumulation has high costs—especially for future generations. Some of the greatest costs are ecological costs to which our Holy Father Pope Francis, in particular, has called attention in *Laudato Si'*.

Growth and accumulation without limits are driving environmental problems. We see collapsing fish stocks and declining wildlife numbers, and lives are lost each year as a result of rising temperatures and its impacts.

Our economic system also has costs for our human ecology in the ways it reinforces inequality. Wealth is unevenly distributed, and the system enables the accumulation of wealth largely by those who already have access to it. This inequality is getting worse in almost all parts of the world. How did we get to a place where the richest one percent have accumulated twice as much wealth as 90 percent of the global population?

We are swimming in what Pope Francis calls a "throwaway culture," a culture of consumption and waste. What we need, Pope Francis has said, is to develop an economics that is appropriate to the needs of our time.

I think today's readings offer a bold and important invitation for us to do so. First, we hear in Colossians, "You have taken off the old self with its practices and have put on the new self, which is being renewed, for knowledge, in the image of its creator."

What is the old self we need to set aside? What is the new self that we are to put on in the image of our creator?

Our creation in the image of God gives us a beautiful vocation and destiny: we are made *for* relationship with God and one another, and not just any kind of relationship, but the relationship of mutual love that our tradition calls "communion."

Situated inside mutual love, or communion, we are disturbed by the ways our society continues to struggle with poverty and economic insecurity, especially in a time of so much surplus wealth. A considerable amount of wealth has been made possible by exploitation, colonization, slavery, poor labor conditions, extraction and more... and these injustices should always be kept in mind and repaired whenever possible. Many have accumulated wealth by sharing in the benefits of aggregate economic growth and must reckon with the responsibility to use those goods in ways that further solidarity and the common good.

Do you feel invited to say no to an economy that pushes for more and more accumulation at the expense of others and our environment? Do you feel called to explore a gift economy, conscious of each other's needs and participating in the reciprocal exchange of our resources for one another?

Or perhaps you just feel overwhelmed by the scale of need. ...We are individuals and families....What can we really do to help move us out of a system that seems to be exacerbating inequality and division?

To this I say that all of us, through our small acts and ideas in circulation as one big community, we can shift the culture.

I recently read about Fr. John Ryan's critiques of what he calls "the higher standard of living fallacy," suggesting that the problem is not simply a matter of going a little bit overboard but rather this whole story of life that seeks novelties and comforts and knows nothing of genuinely higher goods. We need a new story....

Creating that new story will take the kind of ecological conversion that we hear about in *Laudato Si'*....We will have to let go of the short-termism and instant gratification that is so pervasive. We will need to adopt a longer-term view, one that helps us understand what it might look like to live in ways that would make us good ancestors. This reminds me of the parable in today's gospel where God says to the harvester— "You fool, this night your life will be demanded of you; and the things you have prepared, to whom will they belong?"

Jesus goes on to tell the crowd—"Thus will it be for all who store up treasure for themselves but are not rich in what matters to God."

Thankfully the wisdom of today's scriptures can help shake us awake to the riches that truly matter to God—the riches of relationships of communion, of care for one another and for our common home.

Nineteenth Sunday in Ordinary Time

Being a lamplighter for others

JACKIE MINNOCK

Wisdom 18:6–9
Psalm 33:1, 12, 18–19, 20–22
Hebrews 11:1–2, 8–19
Luke 12:32–48 or Luke 12:35–40

We, the People of God, are being asked through the Synodal Process what type of Church we want to leave to those who come after us on the journey of faith. The important word here, for me, is Church—the institution that regulates the faith, and I use that word advisedly. Faith does not change, as we are reminded in the readings today.

"Faith is the realization of what is hoped for and the evidence of things not seen."

As the Synodal Process continues throughout the Catholic world I pray that the Spirit will move and bless us with her wisdom.

The responsorial psalm today tells us, "Blessed are the people the Lord has chosen to be his own."

I often wonder about the choices made by God for me, my loved ones, and the world, be they good or bad. Then I remind myself, who am I to doubt God?

The Lord called Abram and Sarai and their descendants. The Lord called all the prophets and the leaders of the world's great faiths.

We all have a part to play in this journey of faith—in this journey of believing in something greater than self. The process is laid out in today's readings.

We are called to be light to others, using the gifts we have been given. We are called to allow others to light the way for us too.

I think today of latter-day prophets who inspire me—Sr. Dorothy Stang, who worked with the indigenous peoples of the Brazilian rain forests; of Maria Elena Moyano, from Villa El Salvador, who worked against the oppression of women and children; of Oscar Romero, who through the witness of his own priests, came to understand the true plight of those he served; of Dorothy Day, who worked unceasingly to enable those who had little to carve a way forward to a more sustainable life.

A name that may not be familiar to most people is that of the Irish woman Jennifer Sleeman. Over ten years ago, Jennifer called on Irish women to boycott Mass for one Sunday in September. This was in response to the recently published Irish Clerical Sexual Abuse reports, and the treatment of women by the Church. Jennifer made news headlines at the time, but more for the fact that she was eighty years old and had a son who was a priest rather than for the issue she was highlighting.

These people I like to call lamplighters. We, too, are lamplighters. Perhaps the person lighting the way for us is our next-door neighbor, the homeless person, the substance-addicted person, the immigrant, the war refugee simply seeking the kindness of a stranger, or our families and friends journeying with us each and every day.

"Faith is the realization of what is hoped for and the evidence of things not seen."

Perhaps the time space between "realization" and "not seen" is when and where we should and could be most productive.

So let us go forward this week lighting our lamp, being the lamplighter for others and those who follow us—for it was through the example of others that I am here today, believing as I believe that all are equal and loved by God, in whose image and likeness we were created.

We do not know, as Luke says, the day or the hour when the Lord will come. Nor do we know the day or the hour when we are, have been, or will be the light to others or have the opportunity for others to lead us in ways that are blessed.

May your kindness be upon us O Lord as we place all our hope in you.

Twentieth Sunday in Ordinary Time

Persevering in the race

KIM COLEMAN

Jeremiah 38:4–6, 8–10
Psalm 40:2, 3, 4, 18
Hebrews 12:1–4
Luke 12:49–53

I became a Catholic at the ripe age of twenty-two. It may have been the excitement of that Easter Vigil opening bowl of fire and the thick smell of incense weighing down the room, but while we were singing the litany of saints, I had a vision. Activated by our voices, saints appeared out of the parish walls 1990s video-game style, a cloud of witnesses swirling around us.

This cloud has traveled with me ever since. About five years ago, I visited El Salvador through my work at Ignatian Solidarity Network to walk in the footsteps of the Jesuit martyrs and their companions at the University of Central America. If you're not familiar with their story, look them up, but the very short version is that in the midst of a long civil war and government oppression in the 1980s, they spoke truth to power and were eventually killed for it.

For years, I had looked up to the Jesuits and their companions as heroes. They were part of my cloud. But there was a moment when I was visiting the memorial dedicated to them that I came across their robes and slippers and envisioned them kicking back for a football game, not as ethereal heroes, but as humans. They were men and women of flesh and blood, part of the here and now, running the race that was laid before them with their eyes fixed on Jesus.

Dorothy Day, an extraordinary woman and founder of the Catholic Worker Movement, was famously quoted saying, "Don't call me a saint. I don't want to be dismissed that easily." While I was just as excited as many to see her cause taken up for canonization, her words have stuck with me. When we heroize people, it gives us an easy out. They become the video game characters I imagined swirling around me, untouchable, imperfectly perfect. I'm no Dorothy Day. What can I really contribute to this world? But in today's second reading Paul isn't letting us off the hook so easily. Like the great cloud of witnesses, we too are asked to rid ourselves of our sins and burdens and persevere in the race that lies before us, eyes fixed on Jesus.

And so, I ask you, who is part of your cloud of witnesses? When have you dismissed their example because of their saintliness instead of seeing them as fully human?

And what is this race we're supposed to be running? It looks different for each of us—and this is where paying attention to the Spirit and discernment comes in—but the first reading and gospel have laid out some guidelines.

First, we are called to action. In the first reading, after hearing that the prophet Jeremiah has been condemned to a slow death by starvation, the court official advocates on Jeremiah's behalf and saves his life. The story keeps it simple: when confronted with injustice, we are called to respond.

We do this at the Ignatian Family Teach-In for Justice each year. Two thousand students and people of faith spend a weekend in D.C. listening to prophetic speakers on topics ranging from immigration, to racial justice, to the environment. The following Monday, participants take to Capitol Hill to respond to what they have learned and advocate with and for people who are marginalized by injustice.

Students consistently note that the Teach-In is transformative for them. I firmly believe that is because we give them an opportunity to put their faith into action. When we hear, see, feel, respond to injustice, there is transformative potential not only for the world around us, but for our own hearts as well.

The gospel reading pushes us further. Anyone tied to Jesuit education may have smiled when hearing Jesus's words: "I have come to set the earth on fire."

"Go forth and set the world on fire," the words attributed to the founder of the Jesuits, St. Ignatius of Loyola, are emblazoned on everything from coffee mugs to lampposts on Jesuit campuses across the country. For good reason, the phrase is exciting and abounding in possibilities. But the jarring part of the reading—and I think the most telling part of it—lies in what follows:

"Do you think that I have come to establish peace on the earth? No, I tell you, but rather division." Fathers against sons, mothers against daughters. And as I think about the great cloud of witnesses, one of the things they share is their willingness to speak truth to power, some even to the point of their own death.

As followers of Jesus, we are called to make people uncomfortable, ourselves included. As someone who is very comfortable with the peace and love of Jesus, this has always made me squirm. But I find great solace in the fact that Jesus was anxious too. He says, "There is a baptism with which I must be baptized, and how great is my anguish until it is accomplished!" We were never promised an easy journey, race, whatever you want to call it. But at the end of the day, we are called to be part of it.

And so, I ask you, who are the Jeremiahs in your community, in the Church, in the news, in the world, calling you to respond to injustice? Where is the Spirit gently—or perhaps forcefully—guiding you in the race laid before you?

Finally, a word on hydration. Some of my colleagues are obsessed with it. Stomachache? Drink some water. Toe hurt? Drink some water. And while sometimes I roll my eyes at them while chugging a glassful, my experiences with my annual brash decision to run a half marathon have taught me that hydration really is the key to surviving the long race. I once asked a busy Jesuit how he kept up with his life of accompaniment. He said, "You can always tell when a minister's faith life has dried up. They dry up too." There's a reason we are instructed to "persevere . . . while keeping our eyes fixed on Jesus." In order to stay in the race, we must continually drink from the well that sustains us, so that we can walk with the Jesus who loves us and knows us, who hears our cries.

Twenty-first Sunday in Ordinary Time

Striving, gospel style

CINDY BERNARDIN

Isaiah 66:18–21
Psalm 117:1, 2
Hebrews 12:5–7, 11–13
Luke 13:22–30

Exorcism, apocalypse, righteousness, dogma; certain churchy words can just make us—well—sit, up, straight. Certain weighty words might even make us *shiver* a little. Today, in this little snippet from Luke's journey narrative, that word is *salvation*!

How did this happen?

How did *salvation,* the central event of Jewish remembrance, the remembrance of God's saving action in freeing the Israelites from long-held bondage in Egypt, become so loaded? How did *salvation,* which for Jesus so often entailed physical healing from blindness, leprosy, paralysis, or possession, become so *shiver*-producing?

Today's text, with its "wailing and gnashing of teeth," narrow gates, and frenzied, pushing crowds, could have something to do with it. This is Jesus we are talking about, so we can take a deep breath and remember that the gospel itself is part of God's saving plan.

When the gospel confronts us on this Twenty-first Sunday in Ordinary Time, it might be that we need to sit up straight and shiver a little. There is no way around it. Jesus is in a prophetic mood, and he has a warning for us.

The man's question is strange. He isn't asking about himself, "Will I be saved?" He appears interested in figuring out a kind of math problem, the ratio of salvation to damnation. In Jesus's style he doesn't answer that question. He gives an answer. It's an answer without a question. The answer is *strive*. Jesus says, *strive*.

Strive can be a very tricky word.

When I was working as a hospital chaplain, I was called to visit with a young man who was struggling with discontinuing life support for his father who had suffered a massive, catastrophic stroke. In our conversation the son mentioned his angst over the question of his father's salvation. At the end of our visit he said, "Well, it's not like I'm a Catholic or anything and think you can just pray yourself to heaven."

Putting his misinformation aside, this young man was on to something. He recognized that *striving*, at least in a modern, individualized sense, doesn't leave room for God's grace and mercy and healing and love. Where does God's action fit in with such *striving*?

I feel certain that Jesus didn't consider *striving* in this solitary way. Recall the gospel we just heard. In our text, *striving* has something—maybe even everything—to do with being known by Jesus. *Striving* is what deep desire looks like. *Striving* is *our deep desire* to be in relation with the living God. *Striving* increasingly puts us in the right place to see, hear, and respond to God's saving gaze, the right place to be known.

Striving is how we practice prayer. It is how we practice walking through life with our eyes and ears open to the wonder and majesty of the created world as well as to the places where injustice and suffering seem to be gaining the upper hand.

The thing about this *gospel-striving* is that it admits to our unfinishedness. It leaves room, plenty of good room, for God's healing-saving grace. Gospel-striving is not deadly, solitary, or lonely. It is alongside, among, in relationship with, God and neighbor.

On the other side of striving there is always a gift. The gift is finding oneself in Christ: finding oneself, even if just for a few moments here and there, able to say along with St. Paul, "I live now, no longer I, but Christ lives in me."

It is, for sure, a paradox: *striving* only to find oneself *resting* in God; God, who brought the Israelites out of Egypt; God, who raised Jesus from the dead; God, who promises to do the same for us . . . until the kingdom comes.

Twenty-second Sunday in Ordinary Time

Created from the common soil

MARIE ANNE MAYESKI

Sirach 3:17–18, 20, 28–29
Psalm 68:4–5, 6–7, 10–11
Hebrews 12:18–19, 22–24a
Luke 14:1, 7–14

I have little experience of dinner parties where the guests are arranged according to social rank. But I was once seated across the table from the guest of honor, a high-ranking member of the episcopacy. Whatever his gifts as a church leader, as a conversationalist he was dead wood, at least with women guests. He spoke vigorously enough to the man on his right. It did not take long until I yearned to be sitting at the far end of the table.

My wish had nothing to do with humility. It was a longing for comfortable companions with whom to enjoy the dinner. I looked wistfully down to where there sat an interesting Lutheran minister and Rabbi Wulf and his lovely wife, Miriam, old friends from the ecumenical movement. My wish at the dinner party was not a sign of humility, yet today's gospel invokes a similar situation to demonstrate that virtue.

The first reading, from Sirach, gives a practical perspective on the virtue of humility. As is his wont, the author of Sirach aims at a wisdom that leads to both earthly happiness and Torah righteousness. He advises humility as the way to win God's favor. For Sirach, this means that we must not seek the sublime, nor try to reach beyond our strength. Be content, he advises, to listen to the wisdom of those greater than yourself. Practice such behavior, Sirach advises, "and you will be loved more than a giver of gifts." Good advice, whether you are thinking of the kingdom of here and now or the kingdom of heaven. In this context, the last verse seems an abrupt change of theme: "alms atone for sins."

In some ways, the gospel reading echoes Sirach. Like Sirach, Jesus points out the worldly benefit of humility, but he describes it as aiming for the lowest place at a dinner party. The host may well seat you higher and then everyone present will esteem you. Jesus seems to suggest that the pay-off for humility is the esteem of others. Then Jesus turns the parable upside down. He looks to the role of the host, not the guests. In doing so, he expands the tag line of Sirach. When you are the host, Jesus says, invite the beggars, the crippled, the lame, and the blind. This involves more than giving alms. The admonition requires that you associate yourself with those who are outcast because they are weak, damaged, deemed inferior. This is what Jesus did. He sought out the company of those who were powerless and despised—the beggars, the sinners, the tax collectors, the women. He ate with them, and in doing so, he brought contempt upon himself. This humility brings no worldly benefit.

Perhaps the etymology of the word can help us plumb its meaning. At the root of the word "humility" is *humus*, the Latin word for "soil." Not "dirt" which is *sordes*, but soil, as in the rich material in which we plant our food and, even more importantly, the material which the Creator used in forming Adam and Eve. Herein lies, I think, the source of the ambiguity and confusion that the virtue of humility seems to create.

On the one hand, the earthiness the word implies can lead us to consider ourselves inferior, destined to a lower place in the world and in the kingdom and admonished to keep that place. We have seen slave owners promote that understanding of the virtue of humility to keep the slaves in their place. We have seen it promulgated by factory owners to maintain a docile work force, and yes, we have seen women in all conditions of life constrained by this understanding preached from the pulpit and promoted by society. Keep your place. Eschew ambition. You don't deserve to be any higher than you are.

But there is another side to the root of the word. The *humus* in humility can remind us of our common humanity, a condition that bids us to consider everyone our equal, to give alms because the needy one is our sister or brother, to seek the company of the lowly because they are us. And though all of us are created from the common soil, we are made "little lower than the angels," we are made in the image and likeness of God. All of us.

Jesus demonstrated that side of humility too. As a guest, he reminded Simon the Pharisee that he deserved to have his feet washed. As a host at the Last Supper, he showed that his guests deserved to have their feet washed by him. In assuming the fullness of human nature, he became like us in all things, save sin.

If we are to be humble after the pattern of Jesus, then we must assume the dignity that comes from being made in God's image, only a little lower than the angels, from knowing that the Word chose to be made flesh like us. If we are to be humble after the pattern of Jesus, then, like him, we must lay aside the garments that social status and worldly privilege dress us in and wash the feet of those who are like us, equal to us, made in the image and likeness of God. We must, in short, wash each other's feet.

Rarely does the second reading speak to the themes drawn out in the first reading and the gospel. But today in this selection from Hebrews, I think we can find an appropriate commentary. We are invited to enter the assembly made up of angels in festal gathering, to enter the assembly of the first-born, where God the judge and Jesus the mediator are present. This is the eucharistic assembly, the banquet where God is the host and Jesus our fellow guest. This is the banquet where Jesus waits to wash from our feet the dust and dirt of human failing. This is the banquet where we will not be asked to go lower but to draw nearer, standing in the full dignity of our humanity, risen with Jesus through baptism. Keep your place. Yes, and your place is here at this banquet where you will be fed the Bread of Angels. Strengthened by this bread you will go forth to wash feet, feed the hungry, comfort the dispirited, protect the stranger, for you will see in each of them the image of God, the face of Christ.

Twenty-third Sunday in Ordinary Time

Returning to our roots

GINA MESSINA

Wisdom 9:13–18b
Psalm 90:3–4, 5–6, 12–13, 14– 17
Philemon 9–10, 12–17
Luke 14:25–33

What does it mean to be a Christian and what does it mean to have the resources to be a disciple of Jesus? That is what the readings are addressing this week.

I think that some of the language can be a bit jarring, particularly in Luke. Jesus says we must hate our mothers and fathers, siblings, spouse, children. However, he doesn't mean that we need to literally hate the people we love the most; instead, he calls us to reject the power structures that oppress the most vulnerable in our society.

When we think about the Christian tradition and the way it is engaged in our current political structure, there is much to consider. Today, Christianity has become a tradition that is focused on ideas that do not necessarily connect with the teachings of Jesus.

Jesus had four primary principles that he preached: love, inclusion, liberation, and social justice. These are the resources we need to be disciples in the Christian tradition.

What does it mean to come to our communities from a place of love and inclusion, recognizing that liberation and social justice are our primary goals?

This is what we are called to do. In the readings, Jesus is calling us to deeply consider what it means to focus on doing this work, being committed to a socially just community— one that cares for every person, offers fairness and equitable conditions; one that is economically just and recognizes the human dignity of every person.

This is the task that is in front of us, and it certainly was the task that was in front of Jesus during the Roman occupation. This is where his message is grounded—in confronting the oppressive structures in our communities and how they function to marginalize the historically disenfranchised.

Many of us are in a position in a society where we have some form of privilege—and perhaps even great privilege— and that is something we have to acknowledge, own, and recognize. Our privilege is also a resource. Those of us who are privileged have a responsibility to speak up on behalf of the voiceless. This is a critical part of the teaching.

We also have to recognize that we must offer space for the historically disenfranchised to express their emotions, anger, and grief at being denied human dignity and forced into power structures that perpetuate their oppression.

When Jesus says you need to have all of the resources to be a disciple and that you need to be "all in," what does this mean? First, I think we need to be honest with ourselves and acknowledge that being "all in" is rare—it is challenging and a great risk that many of us are not willing to take. That said, what we can do is wake up every morning and acknowledge our position in the world, our abilities to contribute to positive social change, and do our best to make that change happen. We are not always going to be successful; but it is our intention that matters.

We need to dig deep within ourselves and recall the four principles of Jesus's teachings and consider how we can enact these in the world. To love our neighbor means that we need to actually know who our neighbor is and what they need and want so that we can live out the Christian tradition.

This is what we are called to, this is how we can actively participate in our roles as human beings: to make humanity the greatest cause; to acknowledge that every life has value and that we are called to be the change.

We often think that as individuals we don't have the ability to have an impact. But the truth is that it is the acts of individuals—the smallest acts carried out with the greatest love—that transform our communities.

Moving forward we must consider what the greatest issues are and how we can go about addressing them. How can we be good neighbors and how can we engage our communities from a position of love and inclusion with the purpose of creating liberative and socially just spaces? How can we honor the word "love" in a mindful way rather than leaving it to become a hollow term carelessly spoken without intention? How will we wake up each morning and what will we challenge ourselves to do with each day?

This is what Jesus is calling us to do. This is what it means to be a Christian and to have the resources to be a disciple. We must return to the roots of the tradition and demand that the life of every living being is valued.

Twenty-fourth Sunday in Ordinary Time

Compassion makes a way out of no way

LAURIE CASSIDY

Exodus 32:7–11, 13–14
Psalm 51:3–4, 12–13, 17, 19
1 Timothy 1:12–17
Luke 15:1–32

This parable of the "prodigal son" is deceptively familiar. It is ingrained in us that the younger son is "prodigal"—a sinner, the older brother is self-righteous and law-abiding, and the father represents God as forgiving. We think we know what the story is about, but do we?

In Luke's gospel this story of the father and his two sons is a parable, not an allegory. To make the parable into an allegory forecloses the meaning. If all the characters are typecast, as listeners, we are let off too easily, we think we have it figured out. And, this typecasting is also very dangerous, because the parable is not a justification of the patriarchal fatherhood of God. As feminist scripture scholar Luise Schottroff notes, for Jesus and his listeners the parable "does not attempt to give an illustration of the love of God dressed up as an allegory"* but rather would have been heard as describing a flesh-and-blood family—a family in which even the best efforts leave the family disconnected and stuck.

So, if the father in this parable is not God, what could the parable be revealing about God in our being lost? In Luke's gospel Jesus is the compassion of God made flesh. Lukan parables invite us into the world of God's compassion. To enter this world of compassion, let's explore the experience of this family as a whole. If we look at the relationships of these flesh-and-blood people as a family, do we feel the unresolved tension in the story?† The parable of these two sons and their father contains anger, disappointment, longing, relief, joy, resentment, envy—but not resolution. In the final words of the parable, we hear the father's plaintive appeal to his older son to come to the feast, but the ties that bind are frayed and strained to the breaking point—and we the listeners are left hanging.

Don't these family dynamics feel familiar? Aren't these circumstances the very places where we feel lost and stuck? It is tempting to want the parable to spell out a resolution, to offer a roadmap home, to give an assurance that in the end "we can all get along" if we just follow the divine directions. But could it be that parable invites us to experience something better and beyond our imagining—God's compassion right at the very places where we feel lost, vulnerable, stuck, and powerless? Jesus seems to be offering us compassion as "a way out of no way."

---

*Luise Schottroff, *The Parables of Jesus* (Minneapolis, MN: Fortress Press, 2005), 149.

†See Amy Jill Levine, *Short Stories by Jesus: The Enigmatic Parables of a Controversial Rabbi* (San Francisco: HarperOne, 2015).

A woman I know has taught me a great deal about how God's compassion desires to meet us. I'll call this woman "Mary." Mary has two sons, and they are her only children. Her sons have chosen to live on the street in order to take drugs and drink. In many ways her sons have been lost to her. For years Mary has done everything humanly possible to obtain help for her two grown sons: getting them treatment for addiction, providing housing in a halfway house, and working to get them gainful employment. As in the case of the father in the parable, her overtures haven't resolved anything. Though she has longed to, she has not been able to "fix her family" or make it right. Finally, her eldest son says, "Mom, if you keep this up, we will leave town and you'll never see us again." On hearing these words she feel lost. How can she be a loving mother to her sons without working to get them help? Mary has to let go of a plan to make things right and be present to her sons. She has to find a way to love her sons in the real situation, not the ideal family she wants it to be. Now, each month, Mary sees her sons under a bridge, or in a parking lot, or at a McDonald's. All she asks is that when they meet, her sons not be high.

There are so many places where we may feel lost and stuck in our world right now. We are called upon to deal with situations that are unprecedented. Looking around the world, one response to this fear of being lost is to try to impose order and control—to reset the world to what we think is "normal." This is to worship the idols of our own making, like our ancestors in the first reading who have just been liberated from Egypt. They are feeling lost and unable to trust God's liberating presence, so they make something solid, predictable, and familiar. They even offer sacrifice to it.

But the good news is that in this parable Jesus draws us into a world of compassion, a world that is not of our own

making, right in the midst of feeling lost, where things are unresolved, where our best efforts don't seem to measure up. To
be open to this compassion may seem unrealistic—not practical—too abstract. For Mary and her sons, this way of being
present is "making a way out of no way."

I hope we can ask each other, "How do we help each
other experience this compassion, trust this compassion, and
embody this compassion, right in the places where we feel
stuck and lost?"

Twenty-fifth Sunday
in Ordinary Time
Doing justice

MARY J. NOVAK

Amos 8:4–7
Psalm 113:1–2, 4–6, 7–8
1 Timothy 2:1–8
Luke 16:1–13

The Hebrew prophets consistently teach us that because we are God's people, God demands that we reflect God's nature. Since justice is part of God's nature, justice must therefore be reflected in our own natures as well.

The way we reflect justice is through our actions, especially as we engage the systems and structures that order our society. Now, when we engage our systems and structures to create a more just social order so that more life can thrive, we are "doing justice." When we engage our systems and structures in such a way that a less just social order is created, we are doing injustice.

In other words—if we are honest with ourselves—each one of us is doing justice and injustice, because we all participate in multiple social systems. Some are moving to a more just social order, some are maintaining an unjust social order, and some are a mixture of both.

In our first reading, what is implicit is what the early followers of Jesus knew—that their covenant relationship with God, reflected in Jewish law as laid out in Hebrew Scriptures—required "doing justice." That meant creating trustworthy markets, ones that would lead to social prosperity and exchanges that were fair, with a standard unit of measure (Deut 25:15). The prophet Amos explicitly lays out what "doing injustice" looks like in the marketplaces of his time. The markets were places where exploitation was easy because of different currencies; debtors were enslaved even if they only owed the cost of a pair of sandals; and the justice law of the Sabbath was ignored. Amos condemns these practices as they "trample upon the needy" and "destroy the poor of the land." Such practices certainly do not reflect God's just nature.

We see a different form of doing justice and injustice in Luke's Gospel. Here we have a steward who reportedly squandered the rich man's property and he responds to being fired by reducing the debt of the rich man's debtors so they will welcome him in the future when he is homeless. And the rich man praises him.

Doing justice, doing injustice? How are we to understand this? Biblical scholars have found various ways of interpreting this parable without condoning dishonesty. For example, by reducing what the debtors owe, the steward is simply giving up some or all of his own commission in exchange for hospitality in the future. An overlapping interpretation is that the steward lent money at a very high rate of interest—usury—and he reversed that when the rich man discovered it because usury was prohibited by Jewish law. Doing justice in the midst of a just system or an unjust system? Hard to say without more details.

What would be different if this were a situation of a man enslaved, which would have been entirely possible given the language of master and servant in this passage? Were that the case, might the servant have been caught employing some survival method to provide for his family or his enslaved community or even been falsely accused? The clever servant then cuts the debts of those who owe his master and the debtors then praise the master's generosity, making it hard for him to dismiss the servant. Justice in the midst of an unjust system?

The answer is—one that my law students used to hate—it depends! Context and details matter, amid systems and structures at various stages of promoting justice and injustice.

For years, the organization I have the honor of serving, NETWORK Lobby for Catholic Social Justice, has been one of the only faith-based advocacy organizations in Washington, DC, working on changing the tax laws in the U.S. so that the very wealthy pay their fair share. Why do we do this? It is not that we think wealth is bad or that wealthy people need to be punished. We do it because, for generations, Black Americans have been excluded from wealth generation, and thus inter-generational wealth, due to the history of slavery and Jim Crow laws. The tax laws do not tax wealth at the same rate they do income, and this impacts Black folks in the U.S. in deleterious ways.

Our recognition of this and our efforts to change our country's tax laws do not make us well liked in some circles, but after much reflection and prayer, the NETWORK community has discerned that this is what justice calls us to do. The question almost daily is how are we to act with God's justice in a world that, for some of us, is much more comfortable with the way things are now?

The psalm and the second reading really do provide counsel on what is essential. First, the psalm guides us, as does Catholic social teaching, to center those who are made poor by our systems and structures.

And the second reading guides us to pray. We pray for the spiritual freedom called for at the end of the passage in Luke, to serve God and not mammon, the medieval word for the worship of wealth or riches. This is how St. Ignatius begins his *Spiritual Exercises*, inviting us to acknowledge all things in this world as gifts of God which we are to use only insofar as they help us live God's life in us more fully. And we pray that these gifts do not become the center of our lives, displacing God, and hindering our ability to grow more fully into the end for which God created us. Thus, we do not pray for health or sickness, wealth or poverty, success or failure, a long life or a short one, but rather, only for what leads to God's deepening life in us.

This spiritual freedom is how we reflect God's nature of justice. It is a freedom that requires a good understanding of context, good discernment, sitting with the murky complexity, and choosing the best next step toward the kingdom of God, the kin-dom of God, the Beloved Community.

Twenty-sixth Sunday in Ordinary Time

Doing nothing isn't an option

JOAN ROSENHAUER

Amos 6:1a, 4–7
Psalm 146:7, 8–9, 9–10
1 Timothy 6:11–16
Luke 16:19–31

It's hard to imagine a more countercultural message than the messages in this week's readings. In our day the values of helping those who are suffering and being kind to all we meet are not prioritized in our culture. Being powerful, being wealthy, putting others down to advance one's standing, promoting and protecting one's self at the expense of the vulnerable, and criticizing the "other" have become the norm. The idea of servant leadership—that is, seeing our resources, skills, and power as opportunities to serve others—has been lost.

This week's readings give us a very different message about what our lives should and should not be. We learn that we can't be like those in Zion in the first reading from Amos, or the rich man in the gospel, and immerse ourselves in our own comfort and complacency when all around us—near and far—there are people suffering. Instead, as the psalm tells us, we are called to promote justice for the oppressed, give food to the hungry, set captives free, love the just, and protect the stranger.

One of the ways this message gets lost is when we allow ourselves to just settle into our own lives and forget about the people who are suffering whom we may not see every day. I recently had a powerful experience of the impact of forgetting those in need. You may remember about fifteen years ago when the whole world was focused on the genocide in Darfur. Every day the heartbreak of people from that region in Sudan who were desperately fleeing for their lives came into our living rooms on the evening news. But how many of us have thought lately about the people from Darfur? Our lives, and the news cycle, moved on. But all these years later, they are still struggling, living in refugee camps in eastern Chad where my organization, Jesuit Refugee Service, provides education to help the next generation have hope for a brighter future. What does it mean in light of this week's readings that so many of us forgot them?

Today's gospel gives us an answer to that question. The story of Lazarus and the rich man is one of several very explicit messages about how our lives will be judged in the end and the cost of ignoring this message. The message is reinforced in the letter to Timothy, where Paul says that the way to "lay hold of eternal life" is to "keep the commandment." As we know from the story of the Great Commandment, it is a commandment of love—love for God and love for one another. Love for God cannot exist without love for our neighbor.

Today, our neighbors are the people in our own communities who are suffering from poverty, violence, illness, and other crises. And because of the instant global communication we all have access to, they are also people who are not nearby but whose needs we are well aware of through our cell phones, tablets, and televisions:

- children whose futures are forever limited because they don't have access to education
- families who suffer through droughts and changing weather patterns that leave them unable to grow food and feed their families
- communities hit by natural disasters facing urgent needs
- parents who have to make the impossible choice to take their children and abandon their homes to escape violence and other crises, not knowing whether they will be welcomed in the end or separated in the process

I know that when we see so many people suffering in our own communities and around the world, it can be overwhelming. What does the gospel require of us when we feel like we can't really make a dent in the massive need that just keeps growing?

The story of Lazarus and the rich man helps us answer that question. Doing nothing isn't an option. It's important to remember that even if each of us can't solve the whole problem, we can all contribute. And I have seen the amazing difference we can make in our neighbors' lives. Here in the U.S., Catholic Charities agencies and other organizations are helping people meet essential needs and rebuild their lives when they face a crisis. In my own work with refugees and other displaced people, I have seen the impressive resilience of people who were forced to flee their homes and yet, with a little help, are able to maintain hope, provide for their children, and build a future for their families.

Recently, I was in the Middle East and met two colleagues who are among the more than one million Syrian refugees who have fled the war and are living in Lebanon. By law, my colleagues are actually not allowed to work, but they can receive a small stipend as volunteers. They serve as home visitors, going out into various neighborhoods and visiting other refugee families. Despite their own struggle, they are a living reflection of our central obligation to help others in need. Having lived through the trauma of being so threatened that you leave your home and everything you have ever known, imagine how difficult it must be for them to go every day to hear about similar experiences from other refugees. But they are committed to helping. With modest but essential stipend support for their families from JRS, not only are they able to send their children to school and give them hope for the future, but they are able to provide a sympathetic ear for others and respond as much as possible to the needs people have, giving hope to dozens of other displaced families.

There are truly millions of stories like this that remind us of the impact a little help from us can have in the lives of our neighbors. Even though we know that we can't all do everything, and we can't all do the same thing, every one of us can —and must—do something. Christ's teachings tell us clearly that we all need to identify the "somethings" we can do to help the Lazaruses in our world.

Reflecting on the parable of Lazarus and the rich man made me think of a conversation I had several years ago with a colleague who works in higher education. He referred to another gospel story about how we must live our lives—the story of the Last Judgment in Matthew 25 where Christ tells us we encounter him in those in need—"When I was hungry, you helped me," he tells us. And he instructs us that, in the end, our lives will be judged by how we responded, or failed to respond, to the hungry, the thirsty, the strangers, and others in need. My colleague explained, using terms understood in his academic context, "We all know what's going to be on the final exam. The question is, are we going to be prepared to pass?" Each of us must ask ourselves that question.

Twenty-seventh Sunday in Ordinary Time

Increase our faith

SIA NYASARI TEMU

Habakkuk 1:2–3; 2:2–4
Psalm 95:1–2, 6–7, 8–9
2 Timothy 1:6–8, 13–14
Luke 17:5–10

Between 2008 and 2014, I had the privilege of sitting in the Conversation for Social Change Circles as a participant-facilitator. I experienced and witnessed transformation among the participants, at levels none of us ever dreamed of. These conversations were started by the Maryknoll Sisters Peace-building team, which I was part of, and we invited people of diverse backgrounds to have a conversation with one another in a non-evaluative space. In 2010 we held similar conversations in the Rift Valley, one of the regions in Kenya that were affected negatively by post-election violence in 2007–2008. These spates of violence have become recurrent—almost every five years, whenever there is an election cycle. So, people were tired of the pain, almost to the point of despair.

Just like in the first reading, when the prophet Habakkuk addressed his concern to God regarding the violence the Is-raelites were going through at the hands of the Babylonians, the participants in the Conversations for Social Change in the Rift Valley area raised their voices in anguish and complaint to God: "How long, O LORD? I cry for help, but you do not listen?" (Hab 1:2). The post-election violence of 2007–2008 had claimed the lives of their loved ones and destroyed their property. Many became internally displaced people (IDPs) in their own country. Indeed, they had faith, and this faith was tested. Yet, they were able to cry out to God to intervene and restore peace and harmony in their midst. For them God had the power to end the injustices, yet they were shocked that this cycle of violence recurred every time they had general elections. Their resilience was in their faith, just like Habakkuk, who took it up with God and demanded an answer. They too wondered: *Has God abandoned them? How come innocent people—children, the elderly, and women—were suffering?*

Habakkuk reminds us that even when we experience God's silence, God is still aware of the pain and the suffering of God's people. In response to his complaint, Habakkuk hears God's words: "Write down the vision clearly upon the tablets, so that one can read it readily. For the vision still has its time. . . . If it delays, wait for it, it will surely come, it will not be late" (Hab 2:2–3). This was assurance for the Israelites that God had not abandoned them, and it was necessary to have that vision of hope written down as a reminder that God had always been with them. And even now, when their suffering had overtaken them, they were reminded to have something written down, to keep their faith alive.

Faith has an amazing power to transform our lives from a situation of despair to a hopeful one. Faith has the ability to empower us to act, to believe in the power bigger than ourselves that is working within us to achieve a better future. When something is written down, people have something to go back to; when a story is told and retold it becomes part of people's lives, like a point of reference to remind future

189

generations of the faithfulness of God, especially in difficult moments. This metaphor is reflected in the history of the Israelites, highlighting many ways God has intervened for them and rescued them from oppression and suffering. We, too, are familiar with the inspirational stories in our family, community, and nation which keep our hope alive in times of difficulty.

Faith is a powerful image for people who feel powerless, enabling them to imagine a new future, one in which they can regain their power, where they can reconnect and feel whole once again and see new possibilities in the present. Faith involves a prophetic imagination to be able to imagine new symbols and new images that will motivate and inspire people to act in ways that transform structures of injustice into processes of justice and freedom. Faith calls for patience and perseverance, and that's why God insists that we "write the vision, wait for it, if it delays, keep waiting, because indeed it will come" (Hab 2:3). This is the faith that keeps the hungry, the elderly, the sick, and the marginalized hoping for a better future. Indeed, it is the same faith Jesus's disciples are longing for, after having realized that there is no future without forgiveness.

It is not surprising that the disciples appeal to Jesus: "Increase our faith!" (Luke 17:5). Jesus does not give his disciples an easy answer to their request for faith. And the amazing thing is what even a little faith can do. Jesus tells his disciples that if they had faith "the size of a mustard seed" they could command a mulberry tree to be uprooted and moved to the sea. This is an image Jesus is using to illustrate the power of faith, no matter how small that faith is. He is aware that it is when we believe in something that we are able to realize it. Indeed, Jesus is not talking of a magic way of doing things; rather he is talking about the role faith plays in realizing our visions, dreams, and desires.

Any social transformation takes time; it involves conversion of the heart before it translates into action. Changing the structures of injustice does not happen overnight. People need to have compassion with one another to keep their hope alive. Today Jesus reminds us that faith is necessary for a meaningful life. Unless we have faith in God's power within us, it is not easy to live the gospel values of forgiveness, service to one another, and love of God. This is the same message that St. Paul sends to Timothy, that he remain strong in the spirit of faith. It is not easy to see our interconnectedness and the suffering of others unless our faith in Jesus is increased and strengthened. Indeed, to continue with our ministry as disciples, as servants whose service is to transform the oppressive structures in our community, we ask Jesus, "Lord increase our faith." Amen.

Twenty-eighth Sunday in Ordinary Time

The Lord hears cries for assistance

Shawnee M. Daniels-Sykes

2 Kings 5:14–17
Psalm 98:1, 2–3, 3–4
2 Timothy 2:8–13
Luke 17:11–19

In reflecting on today's readings from the Old Testament, namely 2 Kings 5:14–17, and from the New Testament, namely Luke 17:11–19, I begin by highlighting the story about the commander of the Syrian army, Naaman, who had been suffering from leprosy, a dreaded skin disease. Naaman had been instructed to travel to Samaria to be cured by the prophet Elisha, who lived there. Naaman went, and when he arrived the prophet told him that he would be cleansed if he washed himself in the Jordan River. On hearing this, Naaman was angry, saying that the two rivers in Damascus were better than all the waters in Israel. In the end, however, he did listen to Elisha and was made clean in the Jordan River after dipping himself in it seven times.

Our first reading ends with Naaman wanting to give the prophet Elisha a gift in payment for his blessing, for having made him clean. Elisha, however, adamantly refuses the gift.

In today's gospel passage, ten men in a village located between Galilee and Samaria also suffered from leprosy; they all were made clean while following Jesus's instructions to go and show themselves to the priests. Only one of the lepers, a Samaritan, returns to express appreciation and gratitude to Jesus for having been made clean. He throws himself at Jesus's feet. Moved by this gesture of thanks, Jesus wonders where the other nine lepers are. Then, refocusing on the Samaritan man, Jesus affirms that his faith has made him well.

Although leprosy is actually a disease caused by bacteria, during biblical times, any type of skin affliction, such as ringworm, warts, or eczema, was considered leprosy. Leprosy caused victims to present with skin rashes or skin discoloration, distorted faces, half missing fingers, toes, mottled stumps, and/or missing noses. People with leprosy were seen as ritually unclean. Not only socially excluded from Jewish society, they were stigmatized, made to be isolated for a period of time until the priest determined that they were healed—"clean"—or that the disease was no longer infectious, or chronic.

Interestingly, in the first reading, Naaman travels to Samaria to see the prophet Elisha to be healed and then *returns* to offer Elisha a gift of thanks. In the gospel, the Samaritan leper is the only one from the nine who *returns* to give thanks to Jesus for being cured by him. People from Samaria were seen as foreigners. In Jewish society they were looked upon as "others." The enmity between the two groups was entrenched and old. They disagreed about everything that mattered to them: how to honor God, how to interpret the word of God, where and how to worship God. They avoided social contact wherever and whenever possible.

From these two biblical accounts we can draw some parallels to situations in our own times that socially exclude people, marking them as unwelcome. Let us consider people with dark skin color—with Black and brown bodies seen as symbolic of leprosy—treated as if they are ritually unclean. Recent news reports [from September 2019] tell us about Bahamian evacuees, mostly with dark-skinned bodies, people struggling and hurting from the devastation resulting from Hurricane Dorian. Those without visas or proper documentation to enter the United States were made to disembark from rescue ferry boats. President Trump vocalized the need to be very cautious about allowing the evacuees entrance in the United States, warning of the fear of letting very bad people—gang members, drug dealers, and people in general—come into this country, people who were not supposed to be in the Bahamas in the first place.

Let us reflect also on the long, enduring, and pathetic situation at the U.S./Mexican border, where children have been separated from their parents, relatives, and/or guardians. Coincidentally, most of these refugees too have Black and brown bodies. While fleeing corrupt governments, violence, and grinding poverty, they are drawn here by hope in the American Dream. But, seeing them as—in the words of President Trump—as gang members bringing drugs, bringing crime, and so on—our country does not welcome them. While we deport some of them, we confine others in cages, in unsanitary conditions.

Taken together, both of these current examples illustrate the plight of people with Black- and brown-skinned bodies, people who hail from foreign lands and are seen as outsiders, as culturally, ethnically, racially, religiously, and/or socially different from U.S. norms by those who hold prejudices, power, and the privilege to dictate who deserves to come into the United States.

Just like Naaman and the tenth Samaritan, who were socially excluded because of their skin disorders and their otherness, today's refugees have been seen as ritually unclean because of *human-made* purity laws. Many people throughout the world find themselves in inhumane and oppressive situations where they are treated as if they are lepers, ritually—or otherwise—unclean.

The good news is that the Lord knows that human beings are created in the image and likeness of God and therefore are brothers and sisters to each other. The Lord hears their cries for assistance; through his mission and ministry, he erases any stigmas, stereotypes, prejudices, and oppressions resulting from skin disorders, skin color differences, foreigner or unwelcome status, and so forth.

Today's responsorial psalm and second reading reaffirm for us how we are to be as a result of God's constant love, care, mercy, and justice. After his healing, for example, Naaman proclaimed, "Now I know that there is no god, but the God of Israel." The tenth Samaritan fell at Jesus's feet to pay him homage. We all sing a new song to the Lord for the Lord's saving power; for God has given and kept an enduring promise to the people of Israel that all will come out right. From the Second Letter of Paul to Timothy, the call is to remain faithful to the meaning of the paschal mystery of Jesus Christ: that is, to believe that Jesus was sent to show us how to live and love—God, self, and neighbor in a spirit of hospitality and welcome. There is no difference between Jews and Samaritans, disabilities and abilities, men, women, and children, Black, brown, and white bodies. We are all one in Christ Jesus. And like Naaman and the tenth Samaritan, we respond in gratitude, turning to God regularly in prayer and reflection with expressions of thanks for God's mercy and goodness.

Twenty-ninth Sunday in Ordinary Time

Remember, renew, remain, and reimagine

MARGARET ELETTA GUIDER, OSF

Exodus 17:8–13
Psalm 121:1–2, 3–4, 5–6, 7–8
2 Timothy 3:14—4:2
Luke 18:1–8

During this month of—October, in recognition of the 100th anniversary of the ground-breaking missionary encyclical *Maximum Illud* promulgated by Pope Benedict XV in November of 1919, Catholic communities of faith around the globe have been called to celebrate what Pope Francis has declared to be an Extraordinary Missionary Month, by intentionally living out the vocation to be missionary disciples.*

As Pope Francis has observed, Pope Benedict XV endeavored to promote evangelization "purified of any colonial overtones and kept far away from the nationalistic and expansionistic aims that had proved so disastrous"...and

---

*http://www.october2019.va/en.html.

called for "transcending national boundaries and bearing witness, with prophetic spirit and evangelical boldness, to God's saving will through the Church's universal mission."*

So what, we might ask ourselves, is *our* response to the missionary mandate: What does it mean to be "baptized and sent"? What does it mean to "go into the whole world and proclaim the gospel to every creature" (Mk 16:15)?

Thirteen years prior to her violent assassination on February 12, 2005, in Anapu, a city in the state of Pará, in the Amazon Basin of Brazil, missionary sister Dorothy Mae Stang, fondly known as Sister Dot and Irmã Dorotí, a member of the Sisters of Notre Dame de Namur from Dayton, Ohio, wrote the following words to her family and friends, on the occasion of her sixtieth birthday: "I've been able to live, love, be loved and work with the Brazilian people, to help them find confidence in themselves, to profoundly sense God's presence in their lives, and then be a creative influence in society from which a more human society can be born...."

I remembered the example and words of Sister Dorothy as I began to reflect on the scripture readings for today and their relevance for two concurrent events taking place in the life of the People of God at this precise moment in history.

The first event: Today, the Twenty-ninth Sunday in Ordinary Time, the Church celebrates World Mission Sunday. This commemoration itself dates back to 1926, when Pope Pius XI first designated the penultimate Sunday of October as a time to *remember, renew, and remain faithful* as we *reimagine* our commitment to mission and to the world Church.

The second event: Today, ecclesial leaders representing local churches from every continent, are gathered in Rome to participate in the Special Assembly of the Synod of Bishops

---

*http://w2.vatican.va/content/francesco/en/letters/2017/documents/papa-francesco_20171022_lettera-filoni-mese-missionario.html.

dedicated to the Pan Amazon Region. From October 6th until October 27th, those participating in this Special Assembly are focusing their attention, discussions, and deliberations on *New Paths for the Church and for an Integral Ecology* "designed for and with the People of God who live in this region: inhabitants of communities and rural areas, of cities and large metropolises, people who live on river banks, migrants and displaced persons, and especially for and with indigenous peoples."*

Viewed together, these two points of reference, World Mission Sunday and the Special Synodal Assembly for the Amazon, coupled with today's lectionary readings, disclose to us important insights for our unfolding future as missionary disciples. They not only inform and influence our efforts to break open the word of God and make meaning of its significance for our lives, they also invite us to do more than see and judge; they require us to act, to make connections, and to put into practice what we say we believe: that participation in God's mission is central to our lives, that every vocation to share in God's mission involves acts of solidarity and interdependency, of holding one another up, of being stronger together as well as acts of witnessing to what we believe, acts of remembering who our teachers were and are, and finally, acts of unrelenting persistence that enable us to experience the mystery of God's grace, along with the ways in which it operates and transforms human hearts.

As we listen to the story from chapter 17 of the Book of Exodus, the narrative of Moses's need to be supported by Aaron and Hur calls us *to remember* that the vocation of God's prophets inevitably involves the experience of having to be interdependent.

---

*http://www.sinodoamazonico.va/content/sinodoamazonico/en/documents/preparatory-document-for-the-synod-for-the-amazon.html.

As the words of the psalmist offer a message of assurance, they also call us to *renew* our hope amidst uncertainties and anxieties, threats and fears, and to trust in the One who has called each of us by name, knowing that "our help is from the Lord who made heaven and earth" (Ps 121).

We hear in Paul's Second Letter to Timothy an urgent call to *remain faithful* in our embodiment and proclamation of the Word that has been entrusted to us.

Finally, the parable of the dishonest judge and the persistent widow from chapter 18 of the Gospel of Luke calls us to *reimagine* the realities in which we find ourselves and, as missionary disciples, to be attentive and persistent in our pursuit of that justice that signals the coming of the reign of God.

Mindful of the missionary disciples and martyrs who have given their lives for the sake of the Gospel, for the sake of others and for the sake of all of God's creation, let us pray: Sister Dorothy—and all martyrs of Christ in the Amazon, guide us, this day, in the ways of righteousness and peace.

Thirtieth Sunday in Ordinary Time

Our ears listen for the things we care about

Verónica Rayas

Sirach 35:12–14, 16–18
Psalm 34:2–3, 17–18, 19, 23
2 Timothy 4:6–8, 16–18
Luke 18:9–14

Today's readings highlight two important attributes of God. In Hebrew those words are *tzedekah* and *chessed*.

Tzedekah is about justice or righteousness. God provides for those in need. God's *tzedekah* is not indifferent to the marginalized, the oppressed, or the excluded. Rather, God is the defender of the widow, the orphan, and the oppressed.

Chessed, the second attribute, refers to God's steadfast love and mercy. God is *Chessed*, God is love and mercy. Every act of God toward humanity is *chessed*. These words help to tell us who God is.

God's *tzedekah* and *chessed* call us to be an extension of those divine attributes. In other words, God is asking us to take action, to be God's *tzedekah* and *chessed* in our world today.

These attributes of love, mercy, and justice are clearly visible in the first reading and in the psalm. God hears the cry of the poor and the oppressed and responds to their needs.

In the second reading, St. Paul, who lives as an extension of God's *tzedekah* and *chessed*, says that he has made it to the end and asks for strength.

In the gospel Jesus calls us to live those attributes with humility.

The more deeply we live *tzedekah* and *chessed* in our daily lives, the greater we grasp what God is calling us to become.

Like Paul, we need to ask for the strength to continue to live faithfully our calling so that, through the work of our hands and feet, the steadfast love, mercy, and justice of God can be experienced by those most in need today.

Isn't that amazing? God invites us to incarnate his love, mercy, and justice in this world.

Today's readings instruct us to focus on the cry of the poor. Our God is never indifferent to the cries and sufferings of his children. Our calling is to live out God's *tzedekah* and *chessed* in our response to the cries of the poor.

It is like the response of a new mother who hears her baby cry and feels a pain in her heart, a pain that moves her to immediate action; she spontaneously reaches out to hold her child, quickly assesses the child's needs, then responds to those needs.

And even as that child grows into a toddler, teenager, or a full-grown adult, his or her cries inspire a shared hurt and pain. In this sense, a mother's love is like God's love; it is never indifferent to the cries of her child.

Can you imagine our loving, merciful, just God who hears the cries of the poor, the suffering, and the marginalized in our world today? God, like a loving mother, calls us to quick action in response to those cries. This is the truest sense of *tzedekah* and *chessed*.

Today's scripture readings invite us to view current situations in our world not just from a distance or as bystanders, through news stories or newspaper articles, but from a real-life perspective, from a face-to-face interaction—from a place that allows us to hear the real cries of the poor.

One of the biggest challenges we currently face is that we live fast-paced lives that often mindlessly veer in a misguided direction. We live comfortable lives and don't want our regular routines disturbed. Our lives become so hectic that our ears—our hearts—no longer hear the cry of the poor.

One of the great crises today is that the poor and the marginalized are neglected and forgotten. Our ears—our hearts—remain indifferent to their suffering.

Are your ears attuned to the cries of the poor? Can you recognize what those cries sound like?

There is a story about a Native American woman who visited New York City to give a presentation at the United Nations. She had a host, Liz, who wanted to share with her some New York City landmarks. Liz took her to Times Square to experience the energy of thousands of people, the lights from the billboards, and sparkle of the diamond dust in the sidewalk. Alina was impressed by all the hustle and bustle of the city. When they sat down on a bench to soak in the experience she turned to Liz and said, "I hear a cricket." Liz was a little confused. She looked up toward the billboards for an advertisement that might contain the sound of a cricket.

By the time she looked back down, she saw Alina crouched over behind a coffee cart, waving Liz to come over. As Liz approached her, she suddenly could hear the chirp of the cricket. The two of them spent a few minutes in awe of the cricket chirping on the corner of 44th and Broadway.

Then Liz turned to and asked Alina, "How did you hear that? In the middle of all the noise of the traffic, of people milling about, walking and talking on their cell phones. How did you hear the cricket?"

Alina responded saying, "My ears are attuned to nature, and that's what I hear. There may be noises and other distractions in our world, but our ears listen for the things that we care about."

Our ears listen for the things we care about.

Do you know what the cries of the poor sound like?

Not from a distance where we can read about their cries and then tune them out.

Can you identify the cries of the poor in real life, in your hometown, your workplace, your environment?

The poor, the marginalized, the excluded, and the suffering are crying out, and God is calling us to action, to be God's *tzedekah* and *chessed*, steadfast love and justice.

In order to hear the cry of the poor, it is important to interact with poor people, to listen to their stories, and to allow those encounters to move us to action.

Tzedekah and *chessed* call us to critically ask what our ears are attuned to hear.

In the past couple of years here in El Paso, Texas, we have heard the cry of the Latin American refugees seeking asylum. After being processed and given a scheduled court date and an ankle monitor, the refugees and their family members are released to numerous shelters across the city. It provides an opportunity to open our doors and offer hospitality to Jesus in our midst who in the form of our brothers and sisters is fleeing violence and danger. Our Arts, Cultural and Faith Formation center for youth was turned into an emergency shelter. We helpers at the shelters heard the cries of the poor, and the stories are heartbreaking: parents telling of their personal experiences of violence, threats, and murder and the decision to flee their home, culture, and extended families in order to protect their children.

The majority of the refugees did not want to leave their homes but had to make the treacherous journey to give their children a chance at surviving. As the refugees came daily to our door, our hearts were better attuned to understand God's *tzedekah* and *chessed* and that understanding grew in the hearts of all the people in our building. To all of us who ministered at the shelter, it didn't matter where a person was born. The volunteers and the guests shared and lived God's love, mercy, and justice.

Tzedekah is about providing support and about being the voice for those in need, not out of charity but from our religious commitment to be an extension of God's heart.

Chessed is God's steadfast love; it is an interpersonal relationship put into action on behalf of the most vulnerable among us.

Today, I invite you to reflect on our God as *tzedekah* and *chessed*, God as love, mercy, and justice. Then seek a face-to-face opportunity to hear the cry of the poor, step out of your comfort zone, seek marginalized and oppressed people, listen to their stories, and respond like St. Paul, praying for the strength to be an extension of God's life among us.

God is *tzedekah* and *chessed*. May we be an extension of his love, mercy, and justice.

Thirty-first Sunday in Ordinary Time

Speaking to God's beloved

YVONNE PROWSE

Wisdom 11:22–12:2
Psalm 145:1–2, 8–9, 10–11, 13, 14
2 Thessalonians 1:11–2:2
Luke 19:1–10

One day a few years ago I was working on a project in the copy room at the retreat house where I work, and I made some sort of error. I don't recall now what it was; I don't even recall what the project was. I know for sure that I said something aloud to myself, something like, "Well, that was really stupid of you." I know this because I recall very clearly my friend and colleague, Bill, overhearing me and saying in a delightful manner, "Is that any way to speak to God's beloved?" It stopped me in my tracks. We smiled at one another and had a good chuckle.

Now, I was hardly being very harsh with myself. And yet, it was great that Bill reminded me that that's not how God is, so why would I be that way with myself? Why would any of us be that way with ourselves, or with anyone else for that matter, when God does not harangue us? And I do think the voices in our heads—at least for most of us—are not very gentle. The Book of Wisdom tells us today that God overlooks people's sins that we may repent. God doesn't harangue us. Rather, God gives us lots of room to breathe and, with dignity, come round.

If we're not too sure about this, we've got the example of how Jesus treats Zacchaeus. It's a bare-bones story. So there's no avoiding the fact that this short, wealthy, chief tax collector is a first-century revenue man for the Roman Empire—the brutal, repressive empire. He's a known extortionist, charging people far more than they really owe in taxes: pay up or else . . . instilling fear and anxiety in that oppressed society. It's no wonder the people were appalled when they saw Jesus stopping and smiling up at him in that sycamore tree, saying, "Come down quickly, Zacchaeus; I want to go to your home and hang out with you today."

Jesus didn't harangue Zacchaeus. In fact, Jesus didn't rebuke him at all. Recalling the reading from Wisdom we might say he "overlooked" Zacchaeus's sins. And Zacchaeus repented. It seems that Jesus's welcome turned his heart around, or broke it open and freed him, more than any rebuke could have done.

Something in the way Jesus looked at him and spoke to him broke through all the layers of defensiveness, fear, anxiety, greed—whatever Zacchaeus was carrying. Jesus broke through it all, and reminded him of who he really was. Jesus named him as a descendant of Abraham, the beloved of God. Jesus communicated this in such a way that Zacchaeus couldn't miss it and was freed to turn back to the truth of who he was.

And this is what's on offer for all of us.

I listened to a radio broadcast recently of a woman telling of her decision to give up buying new clothes. She has, for decades, loved clothing, and she admitted that she would go shopping as a pick-me-up after a bad day or to celebrate a success, or to calm her down in frustration—in short as a panacea for anything. She came to recognize this addiction and the harm it was doing to her and to the Earth. The woman spoke eloquently and poignantly about the challenge and the struggle.

This is one example to show that, just as in Jesus's time, here in our North American culture today, and throughout the world, we face great challenges. As we grapple with climate change, as we look to the struggles throughout our world; as we hear of further violence in our schools and city streets, and worry about many other concerns in society and in our personal lives, there is a great deal of anxiety and fear. And there are people, like Zacchaeus, and systems—social, political, cultural systems—that cause or perpetuate violence and suffering and instill fear, anxiety, resentment, self-defensiveness, and more. And when we're acting out of those feelings, we're not living as the beloved of God. Fortunately, God is not going to harangue us about it. But God comes, again and again, in small and big ways, reminding us of the covenant, of the relationship with God who, as the Book of Wisdom says, has fashioned everything and loves everything God has made. God, lover of souls, whose imperishable spirit is in all things.

Our God is ever faithful to us and to this world. God is ever reminding us of the promise God makes to all of us, and to all creation—to dwell within us, so that we too can come down out of our roost, and walk with Christ, trusting in the vision God has for us and the world, trusting in what Jesus showed us of how to live . . . how to love ourselves, how to love one another and all creation.

Thirty-second Sunday in Ordinary Time

It's not just pork

ELIZABETH O'DONNELL GANDOLFO

2 Maccabees 7:1–2, 9–14
Psalm 17:1, 5–6, 8, 15
2 Thessalonians 2:16–3:5
Luke 20:27–38

As a mother of four beloved and beautiful children, I gener-
ally consider it my top priority—bullet point number one in
my job description—to keep them alive; to keep them safe,
well-fed, sheltered, and protected from harm. When they
were babies, I cradled and nursed them and stayed up many
nights to comfort them when their tummies were troubled or
they were cold, hungry, wet, or soiled—but even if they
weren't awake and demanding attention and care, I would
often get up multiple times throughout the night to simply
check and make sure they were still breathing. As they have
gotten bigger, I have given them more and more space to
grow, try things on their own, learn to walk even if it means
falling down, and make mistakes that are theirs to make. I
don't hover over them anymore to make sure they are

breathing. But through it all, my number-one goal has been to keep them as physically safe as possible from dangers to life or limb. I'm making lots of mistakes as a parent, but if I can just keep them alive until they are eighteen—or maybe twenty-five, or whenever their own brains are mature enough to recognize and avoid mortal dangers—then I'll have done the bare minimum that my job—no, actually the minimum that my *heart* requires.

Not only do I have a primal, deeply rooted urge to keep my children safe, but a wave of horror washes over me when a fear or image of their demise comes to mind. And so, I must confess and I hope you will understand that when I read this story in the Second Book of Maccabees of the martyrdom of the Jewish mother and her seven sons, my first instinct is to enter the drama and shake this woman who seems to silently accept the torture and murder of her sons. I want to say to her—"Please, just eat the pork!! And tell your poor boys to eat it too! . . . Then run away!!! Far, far away!"

From my twenty-first-century white, Western, Christian perspective, it's just pork, after all. And running away is always an option. Right? Every fiber of my being cries out to this woman: "Just do what you have to do to keep them alive, Mama. Do whatever you have to do to keep those poor babies alive."

And this mother of seven sons is not the only mother who is caught up in the horrific drama of sacrificing her children when faced with the demands of the Seleucid Empire. The Maccabean narrative tells of two other women who defied the imperial ban on various aspects of Jewish identity by having their sons circumcised. They, with their infant sons, were thrown from the city walls. At least according to the text, these mothers did not protest their fate and the fate of their children either.

Now, mothering is a task that takes on cultural specificities in every time and place, and it is shaped and molded according to the social constructions and inequities of gender, race, and class. A mother's desire to protect her children from harm contends with many different threats and responds in many different ways depending on her social location. But it is not an uncommon thing for mothers (and parents in general) to want to keep their kids alive. This is why Black parents give their children "the talk" about strategies to stay as safe as possible in a racist world, and it's why Black mothers have come together to form a movement that protests the destruction of their children's Black bodies by the state. It's why the Mothers of the Plaza de Mayo in Argentina marched and marched for years and years, holding photos of their disappeared children to protest their incarceration, torture, and execution by the state. It's why Liberian women peacemakers used their cultural status *as mothers* strategically and symbolically to demand peace in their country after thirteen years of brutal civil war.

The list of these examples could go on and on, but what is so remarkable here is that the mother of the seven sons in Maccabees does the *opposite* of protesting violence and protecting her sons from the murderous workings of Empire. What is going on here? Unfortunately, the lectionary text for today doesn't give us a clue. In fact, the lectionary text doesn't give us ANY insight into the mother's actions, words, character, motivations, or rationale in this narrative of martyrdom. But the rest of the text of the Second Book of Maccabees does! Reading further on in chapter 7 reveals that she actually *urges* her children on to accept gruesome and painful tortures and violent death rather than acting on her deeper desire to see them alive and unharmed. The author of Maccabees therefore praises her courage in verse 20, calling her "most admirable and worthy of everlasting remembrance" (2 Macc 7:20)—an accolade so great that one would *think* that it should have made it into the communal memory of the Catholic lectionary. But I digress. In verse 21, the author continues to marvel at the woman's courage and relates *her own words* to the reader, "She exhorted each of them in the language of their ancestors with these words:

> I do not know how you came to be in my womb; it was not I who gave you breath and life, nor was it I who arranged the elements you are made of. Therefore, since it is the Creator of the universe who shaped the beginning of humankind and brought about the origin of everything, he, in his mercy, will give you back both breath and life, because you now disregard yourselves for the sake of his law. (2 Macc 7:21–23)

And in verses 27–29, the author relates the mother's words once again:

> She leaned over close to him [the youngest son] and, in derision of the cruel tyrant, said *in their native language*: "Son, have pity on me, who carried you in my womb for nine months, nursed you for three years, brought you up, educated and supported you to your present age. I beg you, child, to look at the heavens and the earth and see all that is in them; then you will know that God did not make them out of existing things. In the same way humankind came into existence. Do not be afraid of this executioner, but be worthy of your brothers and accept death, so that in the time of mercy I may receive you again with your brothers."

If we are allowed to witness the actions and hear these words of the mother herself here, we can glean a sense of why she would not only stand by as her sons were tortured and murdered but would encourage them to flaunt the demands of the king and accept their fate as martyrs. The theological depth and wisdom of the mother's words point to something far more important and enduring than keeping her kids alive. In fact, it appears that her exhortations to martyrdom are themselves an everlasting means of *protesting and resisting* the cruel tyranny of the king and the larger empire that held the Jewish people under its rule. Her words indicate that what is at stake here is not "just pork." It is the faithfulness of her people—her *sons*—to their identity as creations of Yahweh, who called them into being, chose them for dignity and right-eousness, and established the law as a sign of their covenant with their divine origin and destiny.

The law—which in this case forbids the consumption of pork—is not a list of petty rules and regulations to be followed with blind obedience. Nor is it simply a sign of the distinctiveness of the Jewish people as the chosen ones of God. The law here is also a divinely empowered mode of everlasting resistance to Empire, an eternal mode of affirming Jewish dignity and pride in identity, despite the experience of oppression and humiliation under the king.

You see, under the Seleucid Empire, the imperial colonizing forces attempted to do what imperial colonizing forces always do. They attempted to wipe out the culture, worldview, and mode of being of the colonized. According to the author of Maccabees, the Jewish priestly class and their powerful associates went along with this evil operation in order to grasp at whatever power and privilege that they could obtain under this foreign rule. It was the pious and more vulnerable Jewish persons on the margins of society—women, children, an elderly sage named Eleazar—who resisted, who kept the faith, who honored the covenant with Yahweh, and thus maintained the identity of their ancestors. Note that the mother speaks to her youngest son and urges him on toward martyrdom not in Greek, but *in their native language, the language of their ancestors,* for this is the language of the law and thus of the covenant.

And it is *the covenant that is everlasting.* The mother in the narrative professes faith in the faithful, creator God of her ancestors, a God whose creative power would surely endure and overcome the destructive forces of Empire. This text is therefore prevailed upon as one of the earliest sources of Jewish belief in the Resurrection.

And yet the lesson that I take from the text for today is far more illuminating for life in this world than in the next. Keeping our kids, and by extension ourselves, our loved ones, and our communities safe from harm is not the *only* thing that matters in this life. When all that matters is staying alive, we end up going down the path of the Hellenizers and selling out to the evil, unjust, and violent demands of Empire—the demands of whiteness, of nationalism, wealth, power, prosperity, security, and competition. These nefarious forms of pork are a direct violation of our covenant with the God of our ancestors, the God of Jesus and of the Maccabean mother who resisted by affirming the dignity of her people in her own language to the very end. We *debase* our God-given dignity by giving in to the demands of Empire. And we are therefore faced with the task of ejecting and rejecting that pork, of undoing all that which binds us to the ways and means of Empire and severs us from covenant with the Divine, with creation, and with our fellow human beings.

By way of conclusion, I'd like to invite you to consider how you and your own people have, in your own stories, refused the pork or chosen to eat it, resisted the demands of Empire or gone along with them.

What would it mean to reject the pork and accept the consequences in your own time and place—in our own time and place?

Thirty-third Sunday in Ordinary Time

A Sophia-Spirit that converts us

KATIE LACZ

Malachi 3:19–20a
Psalm 98:5–6, 7–8, 9
2 Thessalonians 3:7–12
Luke 21:5–19

Thirty years ago this weekend, in the early morning hours in the city of San Salvador, six Jesuits, their cook, and her fifteen-year-old daughter were murdered at the University of Central America by Salvadoran government forces.

The Jesuits were professors, academics, intellectuals at the top of their game. And they were killed because they were outspoken advocates for those who were poor and suffering in a country that had already been racked by a decade of a violent civil war. Their intellectual abilities were coupled with the wisdom that they needed to use their power and privilege to work for a more just society. They lived out Pope Francis's vision of the Church as a field hospital for the wounded, a poor church for the poor. For doing this—for engaging in the gospel work of bringing good news to the poor—they were deliberately killed. They are martyrs, witnesses to the faith.

In today's gospel, Jesus warns us about what it means to be a martyr. He tells us what will happen to those who follow him, and the words can feel contradictory: Those who follow him will be persecuted, even killed, but not a hair on their head will be harmed. It seems like both can't be true. But we live in the tension of God's kin-dom—here but not yet. What seems like utter loss and destruction here may, in the kin-dom view, be redeemed through the love of Christ that overcomes death.

In today's second reading, the group receiving the second letter to the Thessalonians was living in this already/not-yet tension. The first letter to the Thessalonians held the expectation that Jesus's second coming was any day now, so be ready. But this second letter—tempered with the passage of time and the persecution of the community—reminds Jesus's followers that the apocalypse hasn't happened yet, so the way they—and we—behave still matters here on earth. Our actions will reveal our commitment to the gospel.

Jesus says in today's gospel, "I myself shall give you a *wisdom* in speaking that all your adversaries will be powerless to resist or refute." That wisdom—in Greek, *sophia*—comes from the Holy Spirit—the same Sophia-Spirit that in the fourth chapter of Luke Jesus proclaims is upon him, in the words of the prophet Isaiah, to preach good news to the poor, proclaim release to captives, give sight to the blind, and let the oppressed go free. It is the Sophia-Spirit given to Stephen, the first recorded martyr in the Acts of the Apostles. It is the same Sophia-Spirit that has animated martyrs from Felicity and Perpetua in the early church to modern prophetic martyrs like Sr. Dorothy Stang, who stood in solidarity with the people of the Amazon. It is a Sophia-Spirit that converts us. One of the Jesuit martyrs, Ignacio Ellacuría, said that conversion to God must be conversion to the poor. THAT conversion, revealed in our commitment to loving those who are most on the margins, is the wisdom, the Sophia-Spirit that Jesus promises us our adversaries are powerless to resist or refute. Living out a conversion to Christ visible to us in the face of those who are poor can have profound consequences, as the martyrs show us. But Jesus promises us that he will meet our courageous conversion with his unfailing Wisdom, Sophia.

The deaths of martyrs can feel like total loss—like victories for the powers that be, a reminder of our insignificance in the face of the wars, insurrections, earthquakes, famine, and plagues that Jesus names in the gospel today. But we are a people of unreasonable hope: hope that in the final say, the evildoers will be stubble and God's love will heal like the rays of the sun, as the prophet Malachi writes; hope that, as the second reading reminds us, *how* we are in community matters and reflects *who* we are as Christians; hope that, beyond the violence and chaos in this world—even peeking through it, if you look hard enough—is the reign of God, the upside-down reign where the last are first, the lowly are lifted up, the hungry are fed, and all people are revealed in their fullness as beloved children of God.

The martyrs lift the veil and show us this: Are we willing to look? They offer us a path: Are we willing to follow? And they co-create the reign of God here on earth: Are we willing to continue the work?

SOLEMNITIES AND FEASTS

Solemnity of the Immaculate Conception

Mary and Eve: Giving life to the world

CATHERINE MOONEY

Genesis 3:9–15, 20
Psalm 98:1, 2–3ab, 3cd–4
Ephesians 1:3–6, 11–12
Luke 1:26–38

Today's feast of the Immaculate Conception includes two readings, the account of the Fall of Adam and Eve, and the account of the annunciation to Mary. The readings have been paired and contrasted with each other for centuries.

First, we have the case of Adam and Eve's disobedience for eating from the forbidden Tree of Knowledge. They listened to the serpent, who lied and promised them that they would become all-knowing and be like gods. In contrast, Mary did not know how the angel's announcement that she would give birth to the Son of God could be possible. Nevertheless, she listened to God's messenger and obeyed.

Another contrast regards the sexual innuendo in Adam and Eve's fall. They were naked in the garden and the serpent, thought to represent a phallic symbol, lured them into eating the forbidden fruit, thought to symbolize sex. The contrast with Mary here lands especially on Eve's shoulders, for while

Eve fell into sexual temptation and became the mother to all humans, Mary would somehow remain a virgin and give birth to God.

We need to bear in mind that the accounts of the Fall and of the annunciation are wisdom stories. They contain allegorical meanings deeper than a literal reading of each text. Population genetics show, for example, that no Adam-and-Eve pair of people ever existed. The story instead probes universal questions that face all of humanity. Adam's and Eve's very names confirm this. The name "Adam" means earth, the humus; Adam symbolizes humanity. The name "Eve" means life; Eve is named the mother of all the living, of all humanity.

Their story aims to explain the grand questions all humans face: Why do we live in an unjust world rather than a paradise? Why do we suffer in childbirth or trying to feed ourselves? Why do we always want more than we have—knowledge, power, possessions, and prestige? These are universal questions that confront all individuals and societies. Why, for example, do rich countries over-consume and hoard food, oil, goods, medicines, including lifesaving vaccines, when others haven't the bare minimum to survive?

Over the centuries, Eve more than Adam has borne the brunt of misguided interpretations. The early Christian author Tertullian set the stage for centuries of misogynist remarks. He addressed Eve in a treatise, saying: *"You are the Devil's gateway.... You are the one who persuaded man whom the Devil wasn't brave enough to approach. You... crushed the man, [Adam], the very image of God."*

Unfortunately, Tertullian's misogyny is part of a still thriving tradition that characterizes Eve and all the women after her as weak and deceiving temptresses.

Adam and Eve's disobedience takes on deeper significance when we consider that the word "obey" derives from the Latin word for listening. Adam and Eve's sin flowed from their failure to listen to and trust in God's promise of abundant life in paradise. They listened instead to the lying serpent. They are the paradigm for all of us who listen to mistruths and lies, including the ones we tell ourselves, rather than the truth that resides in our deepest hearts.

God punished Adam and Eve by banishing them from paradise. They would toil for their food, suffer in pain and sickness, and die. Furthermore, God placed the man, Adam, as master over Eve. Note that these are punishments, not good things. Recent theologians, including a few popes, have asserted that Eve's subordination to Adam is a perversion of the original mutuality they shared before the Fall. Sexism, in other words, far from being legitimized by the Fall, is demonized and tied to original sin.

There is a lot of blame going around here. Adam blames Eve and Eve blames the serpent—but note that God, like Eve, places the blame squarely on the serpent. God says to the serpent: "*Because you have done this..., I will put enmity between you and the woman [Eve], between your offspring and hers.*"

In other words, far from aligning Eve with the serpent, as Tertullian did, God puts them on opposing sides.

This underlines an overlooked continuity or similarity between Eve and Mary. Eve's offspring, after all, include Mary and also Mary's son, Jesus. Eve, the "mother of all the living," as she is called in Genesis, enacts God's desire for creation by being fertile, pro-creating, and bearing life into the world.

The difference I see between Eve and Mary centers on Mary's ability to listen and believe God's promise that divinity could enter into our broken world. Mary pondered it, recognized the truth, and said Yes, even though she didn't understand. She didn't need to know everything, as Adam and Eve did. Troubled and afraid, yes: she wondered, would she suffer the same fate of so many other single, pregnant women, maligned as loose and accused of tempting unsuspecting men?

Mary's story, like Adam and Eve's, is also universal. Every generation is beset by troubles: human greed, divisiveness and wars, sexism and misogyny, illness and death. We are troubled. We do not know how to vanquish these evils. How can we believe that God has entered this human world?

But human creation, with all its ills, *can* somehow return to paradise, can become—must become—a place of harmony, love, and abundant life for all.

But how can this be? It seems impossible, although we know that nothing is impossible for God. Saint Clare of Assisi, among others, proposes that we look to Mary. Clare observed that although the Son of God was so great that even the heavens could not contain him, Mary's small womb did—and she birthed that divine life into the world. Clare of Assisi taught that we too bear God's life into the world when we imitate Christ's solidarity with humanity, especially with the poor and marginalized.

What is called for is not the distorted image of a wholly docile Mary, but the fuller image that includes Mary's Magnificat. Mary sings: *"God has deposed the mighty from their thrones and raised the lowly to high places. God has given every good thing to the hungry while sending the rich away empty handed."*

Mary's Magnificat foretells of a magnificent future already happening. It is being borne into our fallen world by every person who, like Christ, lives in solidarity with the outcasts and fights for a world of love and justice.

As we enter into this Advent season, instead of drawing harsh contrasts between Eve and Mary, let us stop to consider their continuity as women who gave life to the world, life both human and divine.

Feast of Our Lady of Guadalupe

The women who dared to misbehave

NATALIA IMPERATORI-LEE

Revelation 11:19a; 12:1–6a, 10ab
Judith 13:18bcde, 19
Luke 1:39–47

Thank you for joining me to celebrate the Feast of Our Lady of Guadalupe, patroness of the Americas.

Guadalupe's image is drawn from today's first reading, which features the woman clothed with the sun, standing on the moon. As placid as the iconography of Guadalupe tends to be, her robes gently flowing over her mestiza skin, her downward gaze and peaceful demeanor, the portrait painted in the Book of Revelation depicts the opposite: a traumatic, apocalyptic scene of a woman screaming in pain, frightening monsters appearing in the heavens, the threat of death hovering over a newborn child. This is an important piece of today's feast, since we should remember that the Guadalupan apparition occurs in the midst of the apocalyptic trauma that was colonization—a time when the Americas were beset with horrific violence, war, and cataclysm. We know that in situations of violence, of famine and disease, of trauma, women and children suffer the most—knowledge with which even the author of Revelation was familiar. And we know all too well, in our present historical moment, the trauma inflicted upon children separated from their parents by war or famine or migration or unjust laws. As much as I used to think the hungry, threatening dragon imagery was a fanciful exaggeration when I was a child (safe, accompanied, well-cared-for), it now seems that end-of-days imagery is not only suitable, but most appropriate, for the despair that surrounds us in so many ways. The country and the Church are beset by scandals that prey on women and on the young, vulnerable populations are vilified, people must flee to the desert to survive. History seems hopeless. Despair seems the only response.

Today's gospel provides a powerful antidote in the solidarity of women we see at the visitation. Mary, herself in the midst of a precarious pregnancy, is also moved to travel. And we have a scene in the gospel where only two women speak. Only women. Speaking. No one interrupting, no one correcting. No one mansplaining. No "actually."

Filled with the Spirit, both of them proclaim. REJOICING in one another's presence, in their precarious circumstances, rejoicing in their communion, they are moved to preach the presence of God within them. Elizabeth shouts! She "cries out in a loud voice": "Blessed are you who believed that what was spoken to you by the Lord would be fulfilled." Blessed are you, Mary, for believing God's promises. This prompts a most unusual reaction in Mary: prophecy. The last two lines of today's gospel are the first two lines of the Magnificat.

This story is filled with women misbehaving. Traveling (alone? maybe), being loud, speaking theologically of God's plan for the world. What prompts them to do this, to move outside of the permissible? The Spirit of God present within them and between them, in their friendship and their bond. The bond between women that proclaims the truth—the ways in which women have, historically, heard one another into speech is on display in the visitation. This is the perfect reading for Guadalupe, herself an uncomfortable fit in Catholicism: the wrong skin tone, the wrong representative in Juan Diego, the wrong location (outside the city of Mexico, not in the city center). Like Mary and Elizabeth at the visitation, Guadalupe pushes the boundaries: of what God's presence looks like (a mestiza), of who speaks for God (Juan Diego, still converting to Catholicism), of where worship should take place (on a hill filled with flowers, not the city center that had seen so much bloodshed). For those of you who are familiar with the story of the Guadalupan apparition, you know that two of the most important things she tells Juan Diego are "Do not be afraid" and "Am I not here with you?" Guadalupe makes God present in the Americas, to dispel fear amid violence and trauma, and she does it through the virtue of solidarity with those in need.

Guadalupe is still a locus of solidarity for women in travail, and as the patroness of the Americas she reminds us not to be afraid, even though our situations seem hopeless, and that she is here—accompanying us, rejoicing with us, hearing us into speech, giving us courage in our confrontations with the powerful, preparing a place where we might rest and rejoice in one another.

On this feast of Guadalupe, in this perilous time filled with trauma and despair, I invite you to join me in giving thanks for the women who have buoyed us, who have sustained us with prayer, and friendship, and prophecy. I especially give thanks for those women who dared to misbehave, to speak with a loud voice, to take their place among the communion of saints despite being made to feel they were the wrong color, the wrong gender, in the wrong place. I ask those misbehaving women to guide our steps, to light our way, and to pray for us. Amen.

Solemnity of the Most Holy Trinity

The forever understanding

LYNN COOPER

Proverbs 8:22–31
Psalm 8:4–5, 6–7, 8–9
Romans 5:1–5
John 16:12–15

When I was pregnant with my son, I rediscovered my love of swimming. As a child, I felt kind of lonely doing endless laps, but these days I cherish those quiet stretches in the deep, counting breaths and tending to the smallest details of movement. My son is a now a toddler, and I am beginning to discover my rhythm. A few weeks back I had an amazing swim. I felt buoyant and powerful as my body moved with ease, riding an invisible current, a cadence, an underwater pulse that just made sense. In some ways, it felt like no workout at all, because it all came so effortlessly. A harmonious meeting of streams of motion—my muscles and the water—they spoke a language I did not understand, but the meaning was something I knew intimately. Even now, the enchantment remains.

In my meditations on the Trinity, I found myself returning to this day in the pool. It was an ineffable experience of connectedness. I felt deep wells of gratitude for my sisters and for everyone who taught me how to swim, but it was also an embodied conversation with no words. It was at once beyond my comprehension and curiously, even hauntingly, recognizable.

The Solemnity of the Most Holy Trinity, which we celebrate today, gives us the opportunity to wrestle with this defining doctrine of our church and to sit in the tension of knowing and unknowing. Before we do this, however, we must acknowledge how this element of our tradition has been used as a gatekeeper. In the Middle Ages (and thereafter), Jews and Muslims were tormented by Christians who wielded the Trinity as a weapon of war. Crusaders demanded "fidelity" by belief in the Trinity—forced conversion or death. It is so painful to see how a doctrine of self-giving love and radical inter-dependence has been used to dehumanize. Even between Christians it has served as an impossible litmus test, sowing seeds of disconnection and self-doubt—but do we really understand the Trinity? Who could possibly say yes?

Here's the thing. It's a mystery. The triune God—one in three. Difference is what defines the Trinity. Father, the Son, and the Holy Spirit—God the Creator, God the Incarnate, and the Holy Spirit. It's central to our faith as Christians and as Catholics, and still it eludes us. The early followers of Jesus expressed exhilaration and wonder at God's ever-presence. This was before trinitarian theology was mapped out and argued over. It was a bunch of human beings experiencing God in and between one another and it was transformative, terrifying, and mysterious.

In our gospel reading today, Jesus assures his friends, "I have much to tell you but you cannot bear it now." These are words of profound comfort. And for the disciples, who a few verses earlier had taken heed of Jesus's cryptic warnings, I imagine they were even more comforting! These words of Jesus acknowledge the humanity of the disciples—our humanity—their brokenness—our brokenness—the limitations of their minds and spirits—the limitations of our minds and spirits. These words of Jesus convey to me the tenderness and compassion of a mother holding her child's face to her hands. God holds us in these words, saying, "I see you. I delight in sharing myself with you. You are holy and the Spirit will nourish you as you go."

In higher education, a place where "knowing" is taken for granted as the universal default and preferred setting, this message from Jesus offers a twist. No amount of studying can prepare you for this journey. It's kind of out of your hands. Jesus has already decided, "You cannot bear it now." Patience and surrendering are their own spiritual disciplines, but I see them as also a means to disentangle self-worth from productivity. You are worthy and whole just as you are in this moment—not after you figure it all out, obtain the internship, pass the entrance exam, or lose fifteen pounds—nope, you are worthy and whole just as you are. The rest, all that is to come, will unfold in time and in trust in the Spirit.

Many of us lead hyper-scheduled lives but the Spirit—she's spontaneous and playful. She nudges us so we may glorify God's beautiful and diverse creation. In our first reading from Proverbs, Lady Wisdom (who may also be read as the Spirit) is dancing in the heavens, cheering on God. Her voice and her body inspire and cajole divine delight. God loves it. I'd say Lady Wisdom is God's pump-up song but it's way more reciprocal than that. They are in cahoots, co-conspirators bringing one another into greater fullness by being in relationship. Joyous, creative, in an inter-dependent, time-insensitive relationship.

Spiritual work is hard work. It often means slogging through infuriatingly winding paths, with unexpected highs and lows—and blahs. Though it may feel like false starts and dead ends—it is just part of the journey. That is spiritual life. In his book *The Divine Dance*, Richard Rohr adds texture to the relationship between journey and mystery. He says that it is not that the mystery is something we cannot understand, it's that we are forever understanding it. My friends, this Trinity Sunday, I invite you to dwell in this reframing of mystery—the forever understanding—and marinate in one or two of these provocations:

How might unity in multiplicity inspire us to be in solidarity with people of other faiths or no faith?

In the spirit of the liturgical year, which calls us to re-encounter our tradition and story in cycles, how have joy and sorrow from your past year redefined your relationship to the Trinity?

How might we use the Trinity as a way to deepen our work for justice, honoring difference and diversity as holy?

And lastly, how might we make space to listen to and carouse with the Spirit, allowing everyday sacramental moments to break open our faith so we may remember, once again—in body and spirit—that God is a verb?

Solemnity of the Body and Blood of Christ

The absurdity of real presence

JENNY WIERTEL

Genesis 14:18–20
Psalm 110:1, 2, 3, 4
1 Corinthians 11:23–26
Luke 9:11b–17

Today we celebrate the Solemnity of the Most Holy Body and Blood of Christ. We celebrate the absurdity of Christ's work—that he took on our flesh and became our food. That God is here all around us, in word, in sacrament, in loaves, and in fishes. Our gospel reminds us that Christ is not just present, but Christ sustains us. Christ feeds us with both spiritual food and corporal food. He fed his crowd spiritual food—teachings about the kingdom, but also bodily food—he offered them loaves and fishes because they were hungry. This gospel account shows us how spiritual work can never be separated from corporal work. They are perfectly one in the same: Jesus's spiritual miracle of multiplication is the corporal work of feeding the five thousand. When the five thousand share the little bit that they can, Jesus gives himself to fill the gap, transforming scraps into an abundant feast. As we eat the flesh of Christ, we become what we receive. We become Christ's hands and feet and are tasked with continuing his work on earth.

This task of discipleship feels daunting today in a world that is plagued by violence. It can be comforting to look for the Most Holy Body and Blood of Christ in the Eucharist, but do we also look for the Holy Body and Blood of Christ in our neighbor? Whose bodies do we fail to honor as holy? If we are to follow the example of Christ, we cannot separate the true, holy presence of Christ in the Eucharist from the true, holy presence of Christ in our neighbor. Who around you is hungry? What are they hungry for? What are you able to share with them?

And what about when we fail? Because we will fail. Our limited, finite bodies cannot do it all. Even the crowds in the gospel struggled to feed each other at first. Here in Phoenix, Arizona, thousands suffer in the heat without shelter, without water, without consistent food. The vast darkness in the world can feel so overwhelming. What shall we cling to?

During World War I, soldiers who did not understand why they were being asked to fight and die would sit in the trenches and sing this song: "We're here because we're here because we're here. We're here because we're here because we're here." The song was a lament of the absurd meaninglessness of it all, a lamentation that there is no answer to the age-old question of "Why?" This song is still sung today, and paradoxically, as the song is sung, it becomes a proclamation of radical presence and solidarity. There may never be any answers to the tragedy of war, violence, and evil, but we're here because we're here because we're here. And today, as we celebrate the feast of Corpus Christi, we proclaim that not only are we here, but something bigger is here. Jesus is here, in the bread and the cup, in our neighbor, in us. In the face of meaninglessness, being here means something. Christ meets the absurdity of violence with the absurdity of real presence.

And so that is what we can cling to, as war rages on and death continues around us, we can cling to real presence: in bread, in cup, in each other. Paul reminds us in our second reading today that "as often as you eat this bread and drink the cup, you proclaim the death of the Lord until he comes." We proclaim that Christ is present, living and dying in each person affected by violence. And we lament this. We proclaim our own complicity in this senseless sin. But, as we accept the grace of Christ's body in our Eucharist, we do not let sin get the final say. What an absurd faith we have—a faith that proclaims the transformation of such simple bread and wine into an expansive mystery of darkness, death, grace, and gift. A faith that God is present in our food—that God is present in us.

And so, in the face of darkness, we can remember these mysteries. We can continue to offer the little bit that we are able to—food for the hungry, clothing for the naked, a listening ear for a friend who is struggling, forgiveness to a neighbor—corporal and spiritual works of mercy. Sometimes all we can offer is presence, the fact that we are here. We can sit beside a friend who is suffering, we can continue to offer prayers for those affected by violence, near and far. We can continue to show up, and when this presence might feel meaningless and hopeless, we can remember this story where Jesus took the little bit that we could offer and filled the gap, multiplying it into more than enough. We proclaim that Jesus can transform even death and darkness. We can cling to the hope that Jesus can do so again. This is our faith. How absurd. How beautiful.

Feast of St. Mary of Magdala

Pillars in the world

Kayla August

Song of Songs 3:1–4b or 2 Corinthians 5:14–17
Psalm 63:2, 3–4, 5–6, 8–9
John 20:1–18

While scrolling through Instagram recently, I ran across a phrase that struck me....

"Wanna manifest something in the world? Put it on the mind of a woman that loves you."

These powerful words didn't strike just me but also members of the Instagram community, who commented on the feed, saying, "Preach, say it again, you got that right...."

It's not just something that resonated with us, it's also what Jesus did.

IN FACT, in one particular woman... we see this echoed truth, *in the first person to ever preach the good news*... we see a woman whose love stood the test of time.

Mary Magdalene, the feast we celebrate today.

We see it from the moment she is introduced in chapter 8 of Luke's Gospel. She was the woman from whom seven demons had gone out. Demons that had controlled her life, clouded her mind, darkened her days, and haunted her nights. Demons that had invaded her soul and imprisoned her heart... A woman who knew doubt, fear, and hopelessness in faith...

A woman who struggled to bring light in, until Jesus called the demons out.

An act of love that changed the way she lived.

A love that inspired her life. Mary Magdalene believed in Jesus so much that she provided for him on the journey. We learn in Luke that she funded his journey. She gave her resources and life to the mission.... *This living miracle of God gave witness* with all she had, knowing all he had done for her and in faith knowing what he could do for others who also needed to be reintroduced to the light of God.

Mary did not only stick by his side as he preached to the crowds, healed the sick.... But she loved him so much that she did not leave his side... even in HIS darkest moment. ... She was a woman who...

- stood at the foot of the cross

- was there when he breathed his last breath

- was there when they laid him in the tomb

- went back with spices to anoint the body for proper burial

- was THE one left crying when everyone was gone

This woman, who had once been a miracle, was the one Jesus chose to be the first to proclaim the gospel! Because when you... *"wanna manifest something in the world, put it on the mind of a woman that loves you."*

She loved Jesus! And he loved her.

In this gospel we see a love so strong that Mary remains at the point of heartbreak. She waits and weeps by the tomb of the one she loved.

In this difficult moment, when other disciples take off, she remains.

We see as he calls out her name ... and she responds to him saying, "Rabboni"—not just Rabbi, teacher, but more specifically, "Rab-BO-ni" or "My Teacher." Not simply a title of respect, but one of care. Jesus was not just a teacher in her life, but "hers" ... one she loved.

The teacher who had opened her eyes to the scripture in new ways,

the teacher who had invited her to join them on the journey,

the teacher who taught her to believe in the unbelievable,

the teacher who taught her faith in time of doubt,

the teacher who showed her love when others pushed her aside,

the teacher who taught her she was not only worthy of love but worthy of God.

These lessons transformed her life and, even after death, they were lessons that would continue to transform others.

In this passage, we see the beauty of Mary, called Magdalene! The name *magdalene* comes from a Hebrew word meaning fortress, temple, stronghold ... something that cannot be torn down ... something unbending, unbreakable, steady and strong.

Mary called Magdalene was the pillar that stayed grounded by the tomb even when others went away. A pillar that could not be shaken. That's what pillars do.

In fact, she is a pillar that still stands.

I recently had the opportunity to travel to the Holy Land with a group of students. They visited Magdala, hometown of Mary Magdalene. It features a church dedicated to Mary with an atrium of eight pillars, six of which represent women in the Bible who followed Jesus: Mary Magdalene, Susana, and Joanna, who funded his journey; Mary and Martha, sisters of

Lazarus, and dear friends of Jesus; the mother of James and John; and Simon Peter's mother-in-law, Mary, wife of Cleopas.

Six of the pillars are named and known. But there are two pillars with no specific name. One is dedicated to the many other women who followed and supported Jesus, such as the Samaritan woman who sat by the well in conversation with Jesus; the Canaanite woman who was called by Jesus "a woman of great faith"; the woman who rustled through the crowd just to touch the hem of his garment and be healed; Veronica, who wiped his face as he carried the cross to his death; the women who wept in empathy as he struggled under the cross's weight; the women who continued on after his death . . . like Phoebe, the deaconess of Paul who carried his letter to the Romans; and, of course, his mother Mary's courageous "yes" that began the journey. Each of them, like Mary Magdalene, a pillar.

The final pillar, number eight, is also unmarked. It is a pillar that represents the women of all time who love God and live by faith, a pillar of disciples yet to come . . . the pillars of community who stand around us today.

It stands as a reminder of the female pillars of our church: strongholds of faith and love, fortresses of God's truth, women whose names we may not know, who stand up and support us in ways we cannot repay.

We acknowledge the way they hold up the Church and our lives! The way they give strength to the body and aid us in finding strength in one another . . . even when the weight of the world seems too much to carry and the roof may be caving in. They stand strong. The Magdalenes of today.

Because Jesus knew . . . if you "*Wanna manifest something in the world, put it on the mind of a woman that loves you.*"

Mary is our example of a woman who knew Christ in her life and loved him with all her heart.

Mary, called Magdalene, a stronghold of the past who

knew the good: The miracles he'd done, the stories he'd told, the lessons he'd taught, and the lives he'd forever change.

She also knew the bad: the beatings he endured, the accusations he'd accrued, the struggle he'd undergone . . . and the last breath he breathed.

So, when Jesus first appeared after his resurrection, he could have chosen anyone. But he first placed his mission in the mouth of a woman who loved him.

A woman who couldn't wait to tell the world and manifest this good news for everyone to hear.

Jesus spoke to this under-recognized pillar of the community . . . the message of hope. She had seen the Risen Lord and he sent her forth to spread the news. From the tomb until she reached the first apostles, Mary WAS the Church. . . . She was the only one who knew the gospel truth and she sprang forth with the message. The "apostle to the apostles."

She was sent to make known that the one she loved . . . LIVED.

She wasn't just a woman who hoped and prayed, who waited and wept, she was a woman who LOVED. And a God who is LOVE knows that a woman *who loves and believes* . . . is the way to change the world.

So, let Magdalene be a reminder of what we can endure, what we can bring, and what awaits those powered by love.

Let us not forget the love that transforms and the faith that sets the future in motion.

Pillars who work, and toil, and pray, and dream, who hope in future and heal in the present. Those who LOVE GOD and manifest a brighter future for our Church.

Who are those pillars of your community? If you don't know them, become them. Because Jesus is waiting, as others weep, to reveal the glory yet to come. Jesus has good news to share and he's ready to USE YOU to . . . tell it to the world.

Solemnity of the Assumption of Mary

There she goes for all of us

Carolyn Osiek, RSCJ

Revelation 11:19a; 12:1–6a, 10ab
Psalm 45:10, 11, 12, 16
1 Corinthians 15:20–27
Luke 1:39–56

The feast of the Assumption means that Mary is just as good as the guys.

There is Jesus, of course, and we tend to talk about his *ascension* and Mary's *assumption*, as if he did it on his own and she needed some help. But if you look carefully at a good translation of the story of Jesus's ascension in Acts 1:9, you will see that he too was lifted up and received into heaven on a cloud.

But Jesus and Mary are by no means the first to have been thought to go up out of this life to somewhere up there where God is. You will of course remember Elijah and his fiery chariot in 2 Kings 11. Even before him, Enoch was taken up by God and seen no more (Gen 5:24).

It's not only biblical figures who were believed to be taken up to heaven, however. Livy reported this of Romulus, one of the mythic founders of Rome. Roman emperors were depicted as having been taken up that way: Emperors Augustus, Titus, and Constantine among them. Emperor Antoninus Pius and his wife Faustina are depicted heading for heaven, held up by a nude adult male winged figure (with fig leaf added in the Renaissance), on a massive column base in the garden of the Vatican Museum. Even one imperial woman got her own depiction of being conveyed to heaven: Sabina, wife of the emperor Hadrian. So the ascension of Jesus and the assumption of Mary are by no means unique. Rather, they conveyed a message to their world: Jesus and Mary rate with the great ones. The tradition of including Mary is surprisingly early, possibly late fourth or for sure early fifth century.

We might be tempted to think of a feast like this as quiet and peaceful, a time for calm rejoicing. Maybe the image in your mind is the assumption of Mary by Murillo, a very common one. Mary quietly joins her hands and looks upward, blue mantle flying, while a bunch of chubby little angels push her cloud heavenward.

But no. Our readings for the feast suggest something different. Being with the great ones isn't peaceful; it means struggle. In our first reading from Revelation, the dragon threatens the life of the child. His mother must flee to protect him, like so many immigrant and refugee mothers, whose children are not rescued at the last moment as this one is. It's a struggle for survival for this woman and her child, a reflection of the struggle that continues age after age in our world.

The familiar gospel reading from Luke portrays Mary as she journeys to visit her pregnant cousin, Elizabeth, and the encounter of the two expectant mothers and their as-yet unborn sons. Mary's response is the ecstatic song that we usually call the Magnificat. Those who pray Evening Prayer regularly recite this canticle, and perhaps familiarity makes us numb to its promises and its threats.

Mary's song is not peaceful. Rather, it is unsettling. It proclaims the upheaval of quiet lives. The proud will be scattered.

The mighty will be cast down from their thrones. And the "lowly"—the connotation of the word in Greek, the *tapeinoi*, means "pressed down," or oppressed, not those who practice the virtue of humility—they will be raised up, and the hungry will be "filled with good things." So look out, you who sit on thrones of worldly power!

Now the problem with this is that in Luke's Gospel it's all in the past tense, as if it has already happened. A quick look around our world today prompts the wonderment: What? Let's leave that question for a moment and go to the second reading, which I skipped earlier because I think it's better to deal with it last. In 1 Corinthians 15, Paul is grappling with his attempt to explain the mystery of the Resurrection to people who apparently were pretty skeptical about the idea. Paul too speaks of a struggle. In the end, Christ will hand over everything to God his Father, once he has "put all his enemies under his feet," an allusion to Psalm 110:1, which had already been considered to refer to the Messiah.

But, says Paul, "The last enemy to be destroyed is death." The Resurrection of Christ has begun to put that defeat of death in motion. We're not there yet, and that's why Luke's Mary in her Magnificat can see from the same perspective that Paul sees here: that last enemy will be destroyed, and when that happens, that's when we can say that all God's promises have been accomplished.

So why celebrate the feast of the Assumption of Mary? Because of what it promises. Mary too is caught up in this great process of realizing the effects of the Resurrection. It's not a promise of peace during the course of the process; rather, it's a promise of tension and struggle. We live in time and we touch eternity.

I have a favorite poem that speaks to me of all of this: G. K. Chesterton's "Regina Angelorum," about the Assumption of Mary. I share with you its last two verses, as Mary explores her new heavenly home.

But ever she walked till away in the last high places,
One great light shone
From the pillared throne of the king of all the
  country
Who sat thereon;
And she cried aloud as she cried under the gibbet
For she saw her son.

Our Lady wears a crown in a strange country,
The crown he gave,
But she has not forgotten to call to her old
  companions
To call and crave;
And to hear her calling (one) might arise and
  thunder
On the doors of the grave.

        (G. K. Chesterton, 1925)

Solemnity of All Saints

Beatitudes people

GRACE SALCEANU

Revelation 7:2–4, 9–14
Psalm 24:1bc–2, 3–4ab, 5–6
1 John 3:1–3
Matthew 5:1–12a

"Lord, this is the people that longs to see your face."

When I was growing up, my mom would often share with me her active dreams of my *lola,* which is the word for grandmother in Tagalog. At the breakfast table, my mom would say things like, "*Inay* visited me again last night," and then describe the feel of my *lola's* presence, the crescendo of shock and then comfort at this appearance, and the message she felt in her heart after the visit.

"Oh, okay, Mom," I would say flatly, all too quick to change the subject. But what else could I say? I was fifteen years old and full of angst. My bangs were curled, my braces were off, it was the early 2000s and I just wanted to fit in with other suburban teenagers. To be honest, though, I didn't know what to believe. Was my mom just longing to see my *lola* so badly that she dreamt of her? Did Grandma really show up? I didn't know what to think.

On this side of life, I've had the experience of friends and neighbors showing up again and again in some of the healthiest forms of community I've been in. Neighbors offering coffee, meals, and care packages after floods; a *carne asada* picnic with the family that once received sanctuary and now have their own home, a deliberate caring for and with the people we honor with our attention.

Just last month, my cousin in the Philippines buried his baby. It was heartbreaking. He and his wife had longed for a child for more than five years. Their son, born prematurely, did not live for more than a few hours. Yet the baby was given a name, a prayer service, and a funeral, and then everyone in the small village where my family is from came to the child's burial. There's this beautiful Filipino value called *bayanihan*, which roughly translates to "community spirit." It comes from a tradition of literally picking up a *bahay kubo*, or house made of indigenous materials, and moving it to a more secure location.

I'm not sure if my cousin and his wife will dream of their precious baby visiting them, but I do know that showing up as a community in a time of distress moves something inside of us to a greater stability of heart. It makes space for other things besides sorrow to live.

Our faith teaches us that the communion of saints actively intercedes for us, accompanying us, advocating for us, and showing up as good love does. In the Beatitudes Jesus described the saints among us as blessed, but so many of the Beatitudes are topsy-turvy, upside-down gospel values that make no sense to us.

The other day, my students played a game of Jeopardy! about the political and historical context of Jesus. Some had clearly studied the chapter I had assigned, while others made wild guesses about the Roman Empire. Later that night, as I reflected on how the game unfolded, I realized the truth of the old teaching adage, "If it hasn't been in the hands, it can't be in the brain." The students needed to engage with the content, relate to it, incorporate their senses and movements, and put into practice some of the ideas and concepts for it to make sense to them, to be real and learned.

So imagine the good company, then, that Jesus kept for him to be able to pronounce these Beatitudes with such clarity. Jesus experienced the blessedness of the people he described in the Beatitudes—the meek, the insulted, the mourning, the peacemakers, the merciful—he joined them at their parties, showed up for them in times of sickness and death, used his voice to interrupt their marginalization, benefitted from their generosity, dined with them, rejoiced in their healing, drew from their friendship, laughter, courage, and example. That kind of lived freedom of Beatitude people makes sense only from close-up.

Now that I'm older, I look more closely at the life of my *lola*. Before she died, she had stayed with us in the United States to help my mother out when she was busy working. *Lola* cooked, cleaned, and walked us to school in the snow. I was too cool for Grandma in middle school and walked a few paces ahead. *Lola* taught my sister and me how to jump rope, tying purple rope to the chain-link fence and counting in Tagalog, *isa, dalawa, tatlo*. I played until other neighbors walked by and wrinkled their noses at our language. When my mother would leave for work, she'd admonish me not to watch TV and to get straight to my homework. I would wait for her car to pull out of the driveway, glance at *Lola*, and thinking that maybe she hadn't understood my mom's directions to me in English, boldly disobeyed and watched after-school TV programming. I actively rejected my *lola*'s patient and generous care.

A few years later, after countless stories of my mom's visions of *Lola* and other deceased family members, I had my own dream. In it, I was back in my childhood home in New York. The neighborhood looked the same with its beautiful, robust maple trees. And there I encountered my *lola*. I was shocked to see her, but could feel her presence, as real as it ever was. I spoke to her and apologized for all the times I tried to trick her as a little kid, too ashamed to appreciate her then. I thanked her for the ways she fed us and helped us with total humility and selflessness. I told her I loved her. When I woke up my pillow was wet with tear stains, but in my heart, I felt both loved and forgiven. *Lola* had come close, and it's almost like I saw with new eyes how she showed up for us as kids. *Lola* was a Beatitude person, and when she visited me as a late teen in my sleep, she provoked and awakened in me the memory of who I long to be, just as any good saint does. Her *bayanihan* of that old, unhealed part of my soul freed me in ways that only love and forgiveness could.

Lord, this is a people that longs to see your face.

Yet so much gets in the way: pride, ambition, shame, centering our own success over collective liberation. Thank God for the ways that community shows up to love us when we are suffering or simply too small in our vision. Thank God for the communion of saints who are too steeped in God's love to be petty and small. They are blessed, drawing us into the improbable ways of the Beatitudes, urging us to choose in humility the ways of mercy, righteousness, and peace.

As we celebrate the Solemnity of All Saints, we publicly acknowledge what our hearts already know in their deepest center: we believe in the promise of coming to life again, of a joyful reunion, of gathering for eternity in a place where we are inseparable from that big, freeing kind of Beatitude love.

Solemnity of Christ the King

We're already there

JULIA WALSH

2 Samuel 5:1–3
Psalm 122:1–2, 3–4, 4–5
Colossians 1:12–20
Luke 23:35–43

When I taught high school, I asked my students to say every word that came to mind when they heard the phrase "Kingdom of God." Then I tried to capture all the words on the chalkboard.

I wrote: "Castle in the Cloud" and "Pearly Gates." And "Angels and Saints." "Heaven."

I broke a lot of chalk, trying to keep up as I wrote more words: "For All." "Everlasting." "Forgiveness." "Love." "Peace." "Justice."

When I would step back and look at the messy chalkboard with my students I would feel awe. Collectively, the students came up with an idea of what God's reign might look like, what it is. They named some of the mystery, and they described the peace and justice that Jesus Christ established through his life, death, and resurrection. They knew, somehow, that the vision of mercy—the mission we were all made to work toward—was about love and unity.

They held the Truth in their hearts.

My students and I would discuss what they had come up with, and why they said what they did. Almost always, I'd hear one say: "God made us so we could die and go to heaven."

When I heard that, I likely made a face and asked them if they were up for a challenge. I invited the students to see that heaven—the kingdom of God—could be the stuff of then *and* now. I'd invite them to expand their imagination—to broaden their perspective.

To expand our imagination and change our perspective: I believe this is what we all are invited to do today, as we celebrate the Solemnity of Our Lord Jesus Christ, King of the Universe.

From the macro of the cosmos to the micro of our hearts: the love of Christ prevails and has authority. Christ's power is real and transformative.

To see this, we are invited to shift our perspective. To step back and see the big mess on the board.

Entering into the Word of God expands our view. Today's passage from Colossians is an ancient song of gratitude, a hymn of praise. Its music is in harmony with the trust in God's authority that is expressed in Psalm 122.

As it says in Colossians:

Brothers and sisters:
Let us give thanks to the Father,
who has made you fit to share
in the inheritance of the holy ones in light.
He delivered us from the power of darkness
and transferred us to the kingdom of his beloved Son,
in whom we have redemption, the forgiveness of sins.

Do you hear it? Do you see it?

We have been made for this: we are fit to share in the inheritance of the holy ones in light. We have been delivered from darkness. And we have been transferred to the kingdom of Jesus Christ.

The words of the hymn in Colossians are in the past tense. The early Church is praising God for what has already happened. And it's true for all of us: We've been transferred into the kingdom. We're already there.

I can't help but wonder: If we believed that we have already been transferred into the kingdom, how might our lives look like songs of praise? What would happen if we lived as if we believed salvation had already been given us? What would we act like if we really believed that the kingdom of God surrounds us? Would we live with more joy and wonder? Would we reverence God and every part of creation we encounter?

I imagine that if we believed that we are already in the kingdom of God, then we'd live more wholeheartedly. We'd be our true selves, free and unafraid of judgments, not worried about fitting in.

We'd heed the advice of St. Francis de Sales: "Be who you are, and be it perfectly well."

We'd show up for others, every day.

We'd love wildly and freely—no longer trapped by the limits of what we alone can dream up.

We wouldn't be stuck in a pile of "should" and "shouldn't."

We'd be celebrating the goodness.

Or sharing bread. Or moving our bodies to the places of power and demanding freedom for others. We'd love without worry about the cost, without concern for how it might impact us.

Because if we are free, then we are concerned with the common good—not just our own tribes or preferences. If we are truly ourselves, we are filled with trust that in this reign of God, we're all safe and loved. We all belong and are needed.

I wonder what stops us from living this way. Personally, I can admit that I get trapped with being concerned about what others think. Do I seem completely foolish or inappropriate? Are people judging me? When I reflect on these questions, I can see that when my gaze is on myself, I am not able to see the kingdom around me.

I invite you all to consider: What gets in the way of your living like you believe that the kingdom is around you right now? How would you act differently if you believed you had been truly saved and set free? If God had total power over you? What gets in the way of sharing the goodness of God's reign with others?

I'm learning that a contemplative life helps us know the truth, to keep our gaze fixed on Jesus and his reign and gain more freedom.

The criminal who gets to join Jesus in paradise models this for us all. In a story unique to Luke's Gospel, we meet a criminal who is unexpectedly humble and names the truth. He understands that he's united with Jesus, subject to the same condemnation. He knows he is powerless, but Christ is at his side. He encourages another to fear God, to have awe and respect. He understands the limits of his humanity.

The criminal next to Jesus shows us how the reign of God can be known and experienced if our gaze is totally on Jesus, on the power of God, and not on one's self. From a cross, the criminal gained a new perspective and was able to see the truth. He was free to be authentic, to see the big picture, to know the love of God.

Following the criminal's example, let us also see the kingdom of God around us and live like the saints we were made to be!

Preacher Biographies

Kayla August
Kayla August is a student in the School of Theology and Ministry at Boston College, where she is pursuing a PhD in theology and education with a focus on preaching, particularly preaching from the lay perspective. Practicing what she preaches, Kayla steps out of the margins to preach as a layperson in a variety of places and communities, such as McGrath's Institute for Church Life Saturday with the Saints at Notre Dame, Future Church's Catholic Women DO Preach Prayer Service in Support of Women's Voices in the Church, and on an episode of *America* magazine's podcast *Preach*. She hopes, through preaching, to inspire and empower marginalized voices—like her own—in the Catholic faith to play an active role in the Church, because when we are able to hear more voices in the Church, we are able to grow in our understanding of God.

M. Patricia Ball
M. Patricia Ball, M.S.R.N. was born and raised and continues to reside in Baltimore, Maryland. She entered the School Sisters of Notre Dame after high school, but left at the end of her novitiate year to pursue other career paths of service. After receiving an master's degree in counseling, Patricia worked for several years with children and adolescents with severe mental health problems. She pursued a nursing degree

to better serve those with severe mental health issues and has been a practicing psychiatric nurse since 1983. Her current professional work is in the area of research into treatments for schizophrenia. For the past forty-five years Patricia has been an active member of St. Vincent de Paul Parish in Baltimore, where she currently serves as a lector, liturgy planner, and Eucharistic minister, and on the Committee on Church Reform. Patricia has been active with Discerning Deacons since its inception and also serves as a hospice volunteer.

Bridget Bearss, RSCJ

Bridget Bearss, RSCJ, is an educator, artist-writer, activist for the Beatitudes, and facilitator of processes to build and strengthen the experience of communities of dialogue, justice, and hope. She is a member of the Society of the Sacred Heart, United States–Canada Province, currently serving as associate director for Transformative Justice for the Leadership Conference of Women Religious (LCWR). She received her BA in education from Maryville University and her MEd in educational policies and leadership from Washington University, both in St. Louis. She previously served as executive director of the Stuart Center for Mission in Washington, DC, and spent thirty-five years working in the network of Sacred Heart Schools, including twenty-six years at the Academy of the Sacred Heart, Bloomfield Hills, MI.

Cindy Bernardin

Cindy Bernardin has been firmly planted in southern Indiana for the past thirty-five years, where she and her husband, Rob, raised their four children. In response to the nagging question "How do I pass this faith on to my children in a robust and compelling way?" Cindy enrolled in the MA program at Saint Meinrad Seminary and School of Theology. Over the next ten years she engaged in a wide variety of parish ministries before spending seven years as a certified Catholic chaplain in a level-two trauma hospital. In 2021 she received her doctor of ministry in preaching degree at Aquinas Institute in St. Louis. Cindy preaches ecumenical Sunday Morning Prayer once a month in New Harmony, Indiana. Her latest ministry is working as a preaching coach for the Institute for Homiletics—Preaching for Encounter program, a collaboration between the University of Dallas, the Catholic Foundation of Dallas, and the Archdiocese of Dallas.

Cora Marie Billings, RSM

Sister Cora Marie Billings has been a member of the Institute of the Sisters of Mercy of the Americas for sixty-five years. During that time she has been a teacher, a campus minister, and an administrator. She is one of the founding members of the National Black Sisters' Conference. Since 1968 she has been an advocate for human rights and anti-racism. As such she has done presentations around the nation. At present she considers herself a community volunteer.

Melinda Brown Donovan

Since 1995, Melinda has worked in spiritual direction, faith formation, and parish ministry. Raised in the Presbyterian tradition, she chose to become Catholic as a young adult. Melinda holds an MA in pastoral ministry and post-graduate certificates in ecclesial ministry and spiritual formation, all from Boston College. For ten years she served in parish ministry within the Archdiocese of Boston, and began working for Boston College in 2006. She served as associate director for Continuing Education at the School of Theology and Ministry (STM) until her retirement in 2019, coordinating on-campus events and working with online faith enrichment courses for STM Online: Crossroads. A spiritual director since 2002, Melinda continues to accompany those seeking deeper relationship with the Divine. She also provides supervision for other spiritual directors. A native of Colorado, Melinda and her husband are longtime residents of Massachusetts and the parents of three adult children and four grandchildren.

Laurie Cassidy
Laurie Cassidy, PhD, is a theologian, anti-racist activist, and spiritual director. She currently teaches in the Christian Spirituality Program at Creighton University and was associate professor in the religious studies department at Marywood University in Scranton, Pennsylvania. An award-winning author and editor, her latest book, *Desire, Darkness and Hope: Theology in a Time of Impasse* was edited with M. Shawn Copeland. Her forthcoming book is entitled *Praying for Freedom: Racism and Ignatian Spirituality in America*. Over the past thirty years, Laurie has been engaged in ministry that facilitates the intersection of personal and social transformation. Raised in Massachusetts, she now makes her home in the foothills of the Rocky Mountains, traditional homeland of the Ute in Colorado.

Melissa Cedillo
Melissa Cedillo was born and raised in California's Coachella Valley. She attended Loyola Marymount University (LMU) in Los Angeles where she earned a BA in theological studies. After college, Melissa spent time in Washington, DC, as a campaign associate for Faith in Public Life working to defend the integrity of the 2020 Census. Melissa then went on to complete an MTS at Harvard Divinity School, where she studied religion, ethics, and politics through a public policy lens. After earning her MTS, Melissa spent a year at the *Na-*

tional Catholic Reporter as the Latino Catholics Fellow. She currently works as a senior associate at the Raben Group, and is passionate about bridging the gap between progressive politics and religion in America. Melissa is dedicated to learning about and advocating for preventative domestic violence policy, reproductive justice, immigration advocacy, pushing for prison divestment, and decarceration work.

Kim Coleman

Kim Coleman has worked for the Ignatian Solidarity Network since 2011, first as program director and now as director of integrated marketing and campaigns. After graduating from Gonzaga University with a degree in marketing and broadcast studies, Kim spent two years serving in the Jesuit Volunteer Corps. During her years of service, Kim worked with teens with developmental disabilities at STRIVE in South Portland, ME, and served as the outreach coordinator for Jesuit Refugee Service/USA in Washington, DC. Through her work at the Ignatian Solidarity Network, Kim helps develop retreats, conferences, networking opportunities, and resources at the nexus of faith, leadership, and social justice. She is constantly humbled by the authenticity and hunger for a "faith that does justice" in the students and people of faith she encounters in her work each day. A Californian at heart, Kim lives outside of Cleveland, OH, with her husband, Jeff, and son, Jackson.

Lynn Cooper

Lynn Cooper is the associate director of the University Chaplaincy and Catholic chaplain at Tufts University. She holds a doctor of ministry degree from Boston University School of Theology and a master of ministry degree from Harvard Divinity School. Working in a multifaith chaplaincy context in higher education has been one of the great gifts of her life. At

Tufts, she runs an interfaith friendship project for students, faculty, and staff and is currently working on intergenerational oral history that magnifies the wisdom and stories of lay folks.

M. Shawn Copeland

M. Shawn Copeland is professor emerita of systematic theology in the Department of Theology of the Morrissey College and Graduate School of Arts and Sciences at Boston College. Copeland's research and writing focus on shifts in theological understanding of the human person; suffering, solidarity, and the cross of Jesus of Nazareth in probing conditions under which human persons may flourish authentically; and thematizing an African American Catholic theology. Her books include *Enfleshing Freedom: Body, Race, and Being*; *The Subversive Power of Love: The Vision of Henriette Delille*; and *Knowing Christ Crucified: The Witness of African American Religious Experience*. Professor Copeland is a former convener of the Black Catholic Theological Symposium (BCTS). She was the first African American to serve as president of the Catholic Theological Society of America (CTSA), by which, in 2018, she was also awarded the society's highest honor, the John Courtney Murray Award.

Gretchen Crowder

Gretchen Crowder has served as a campus minister and Ignatian educator for the Jesuit Dallas community for the last seventeen years. She graduated from the University of Notre Dame with a BS in mathematics ('98) and an MEd ('02) from its Alliance for Catholic Education program. Before assuming her current role at Jesuit Dallas, Gretchen taught mathematics for almost a decade. As she entered her new role in ministry, she simultaneously enrolled in the University of Dallas's master of theological studies program, from which she graduated in

2016. She is a member of the Jesuit Schools Network Ignatian Spirituality Advisory Committee and a member of the University of Dallas Neuhoff Institute's Alumni Board. She currently attends Loyola Chicago in their Certificate in Spiritual Direction program and will be graduating in 2025. She is also a freelance writer and speaker and is the host of *Loved as You Are: An Ignatian Podcast*. A collection of her writings can be found at gretchencrowder.com. She lives in Dallas, TX, with her husband, three boys, and an ever-growing number of pets.

Shawnee M. Daniels-Sykes (deceased)
Shawnee M. Daniels-Sykes, PhD, who died on October 31, 2022, was a professor of theology and ethics at Mount Mary University, Milwaukee, WI. A registered nurse by training, Dr. Daniels-Sykes received her doctorate from Marquette University in religious studies with a specialization in theological ethics and a sub-specialization in bioethics. She was a faculty member in the Theology Collaborative for Ascension Health Care USA, where she taught an online course on Moral Theology and Catholic Social Teaching for Ascension Health Care Executive Leaders. During the summers, she taught the course Moral Questions in the Black Community at the Institute for Black Catholic Studies at Xavier University of Louisiana. In addition to being a published author, she was a frequent national and international speaker. In 2019, she was recognized with the Black Excellence Award from the *Milwaukee Times*.

Brenna Davis
Brenna Davis lives in a loving community in Cleveland, OH, with one of her community members from Jesuit Volunteer Corps and her cat, Fran. Originally from Tennessee, she graduated from Boston College in 2010 with a BA in theology

and Spanish. After college, Brenna served as a Jesuit Volunteer in Cleveland. When her JV year ended, she began working at Saint Martin de Porres, Cleveland's Cristo Rey High School, as a theology teacher and cross-country coach. Brenna currently serves as the director of Integral Ecology at the Ignatian Solidarity Network. She is a certified spiritual director, Cuyahoga County Master Recycler, and a board member for the Jesuit Retreat Center in Parma, OH, and Bethlehem Farm in Pence Springs, WV. In her spare time, Brenna enjoys reading, long walks, playing ultimate Frisbee, bullet journaling, knitting, writing letters, and digging through trash cans to properly sort recycling.

Teresa Delgado

Teresa Delgado is dean of St. John's College of Liberal Arts and Sciences and professor of theology and religious studies at St. John's University (Queens, NY). She received her doctorate from Union Theological Seminary in New York City. She has published on topics such as diversity in higher education, transformational pedagogies, constructive theology and ethics, and justice for racially, ethnically, and sexually minoritized persons. Her essays include "Metaphor for Teaching: Good Teaching Is Like Good Sex" (*Teaching Theology and Religion* 18, no. 3, July 2015) and "Beyond Procreativity: Heterosexuals Queering Marriage," in *Queer Christianities: Lived Religion in Transgressive Forms* (NYU Press, 2014). Dr. Delgado's book, *A Puerto Rican Decolonial Theology: Prophesy Freedom*, was published in September 2017 (Palgrave Macmillan). She is composing a manuscript on sexual ethics, *Loving Sex: A Decolonial Theology of the Body*. She lives in Mount Vernon, NY; with her husband, Pascal Kabemba (deceased June 6, 2023), she has been blessed with four beautiful (adult) children.

Noella de Souza, MCJ

Noella belongs to a community of women religious, the Missionaries of Christ Jesus, and has been trained in education, psychotherapy, and counseling. She has engaged in the field of education for the last forty years, working to see that all children in India get an equal and quality education. A member of the Core Team of a prominent NGO in Mumbai, she works as a research writer to bring about reforms in educational content and pedagogy; the team has produced unique supplementary courses as well as a Gender Equality kit that addresses sexual violence toward women and young girls. In her capacity as psychotherapist and counselor, she works mainly with women who have problems with identity, self-esteem, efficacy, and worth. As a member of Satyashodak, a women's collective, she has been actively involved in securing justice for victims of sexual abuse in the Archdiocese of Mumbai and further afield.

Colleen Dulle

Colleen Dulle is a multimedia journalist covering Catholic and Vatican news. In her current position as associate editor at America Media, Colleen writes and edits Vatican news and analysis pieces, along with hosting and producing the weekly news podcast *Inside the Vatican*. She creates Vatican explainer videos for America Media's YouTube channel and contributes to Sacred Heart University's *Go, Rebuild My House* blog. Her forthcoming book, *Struck Down, Not Destroyed*, on the spiritual crises that result from reporting on the endemic problems of the Catholic Church, will be published by Penguin Random House in early 2025.

Sara Fairbanks, OP

Dr. Sara Fairbanks, OP, is an Adrian Dominican Sister and associate professor of theology and preaching at Aquinas

Institute in St. Louis. Sara holds a master of theology from Aquinas Institute of Theology in St. Louis and a doctorate in theology from the University of St. Michael's College, the Toronto School of Theology. Sara works every summer at the Dominican College Preaching in Action Conference and the Dominican High School Preaching in Action Conference, offering workshops on the art of liturgical preaching. She published *Fully Human: Understanding Christian Anthropology: 12 Lectures on DVD and CD* (Now You Know Media, 2017), as well as articles on lay liturgical preaching in *Worship* (2003), *Listening* (2003), and *Liturgical Ministry* (2006). She is a contributing author to *Feasting on the Gospels—Luke Volume 1*, A Feasting on the Word Commentary (Westminster John Knox Press, 2014), and contributed two chapters to *Theology: Faith, Beliefs, Traditions* (Kendall Hunt, 2010).

Susan Fleming McGurgan

Dr. Susan McGurgan served as director of lay ecclesial formation and associate professor of pastoral theology at Mount St. Mary's Seminary in Cincinnati for twenty-three years. She holds a BA honors history degree from Oklahoma State University, an MA in religion from Mount St. Mary's, and a DMin in preaching from Bexley-Seabury. She completed three years of doctoral work in ancient history at the University of Cincinnati, and a museum internship at the Cincinnati Art Museum in the department of Ancient and Near Eastern Art. She is active in the Catholic Association of Teachers of Homiletics, serving previously as vice president and president, and in the Academy of Homiletics, serving on the Executive Committee and as co-convener of the Theology Work Group. In the fall of 2020, she was the Marten Visiting Associate Fellow of Preaching at the University of Notre Dame. Currently she is an adjunct instructor in pastoral studies and preaching at Mount St. Mary's and at United Theological Seminary in Dayton. In 2021, she launched a preaching website, Preaching Hope: www.preachinghope.org.

Elyse Galloway

Elyse Galloway, a Maryland native and New York City resident, holds bachelor degrees in anthropology and community health from Tufts University and a master's degree in public health from Yale University. At both institutions, Elyse dedicated her time to extracurricular activities promoting community engagement and development. She currently partners with a number of biopharmaceutical, public health, and consumer health entities and health systems to advance public health and health equity. Matching unmet public health needs to the unique skills and competencies of her clients, she shapes authentic and actionable health endeavors that drive sustained impact and build brand equity.

Elizabeth O'Donnell Gandolfo

Elizabeth O'Donnell Gandolfo is the Earley Associate Professor of Catholic and Latin American Studies at Wake Forest University School of Divinity. She holds a BA in theology from St. Joseph's University, an MTS from the University of Notre Dame, and a PhD in theological studies from Emory University. As a constructive theologian rooted in the Catholic tradition, her teaching and research place Christian theology in conversation with human responses to vulnerability, suffering, violence, and oppression, especially in contexts of social injustice and ecological degradation. Dr. Gandolfo is author of *The Power and Vulnerability of Love: A Theological Anthropology* (Fortress, 2015), co-editor of *Parenting as Spiritual Practice and Source for Theology: Mothering Matters* (Palgrave Macmillan, 2017), co-author of *Re-membering the Reign of God: The Decolonial Witness of El Salvador's Church of the Poor* (Lexington, 2022), and author of *Ecomartyrdom in the Americas: Living and Dying for Our Common Home* (Orbis Books, 2023).

Elizabeth Garlow

Elizabeth Garlow has worked in the areas of social entrepreneurship, impact investing, and public policy with an eye toward building an economy rooted in solidarity and mutual care. Elizabeth is a co-founder of the Francesco Collaborative, a network of investors, entrepreneurs, and other changemakers seeking to respond to Pope Francis's call to be "protagonists of transformation" in our economy. She runs "Livable Future Investing" workshops, inviting investors to discern and embrace their most important work in building the solidarity economy. She accompanies religious congregations as they discern how to align their assets with mission in an ever-evolving world. She also conducts research on well-being economics as a fellow with New America. Elizabeth holds a BA from Kalamazoo College and a master's in public policy and economics from Princeton University. She loves swimming, playing folk music, and making a home in the Detroit area with her partner, Paul, and their daughter, Sophia.

Ann Garrido

Ann Garrido is associate professor of homiletics at the Aquinas Institute in St. Louis, MO. In 2018, she served as the Marten Fellow in Preaching at the University of Notre Dame. Ann preaches each month for Word.op.org and is one of the core homilists for the Preaching and the Sciences project sponsored by the John Templeton Foundation. She is the author of several award-winning books, including *Redeeming Administration* (Ave Maria Press, 2013), *Redeeming Conflict* (Ave Maria Press, 2016), *Let's Talk about Truth* (Ave Maria

Press, 2020), #*Rules of Engagement* (Ave Maria Press, 2021), and *Preaching with Children* (Liturgy Training Publications, 2022). Her newest book is *Redeeming Power* (Ave Maria Press, 2024).

Colleen Gibson, SSJ

Sister Colleen Gibson is a Sister of Saint Joseph who currently serves as coordinator of pastoral care at St. John–St. Paul Catholic Collaborative in Wellesley, MA. A member of the founding ministry team at the Sisters of Saint Joseph Neighborhood Center in Camden, New Jersey, Sister Colleen is co-host of the podcast *Beyond the Habit* and a regular contributor to *Give Us This Day*, *National Catholic Reporter*, and *Global Sisters Report*. In addition to her writing, Sister Colleen shares her gifts as a speaker and retreat director, inviting participants to explore issues of call, spirituality, and culture from an Ignatian perspective. Prior to her work at the SSJ Neighborhood Center, Sister Colleen served as a campus minister at Chestnut Hill College. She holds a master of theological studies degree from Boston College School of Theology and Ministry and a bachelor of arts degree in American studies and religious studies from Fairfield University.

Cecilia González-Andrieu

Cecilia González-Andrieu is professor of theology at Loyola Marymount University, where she also works on multiple initiatives to serve the Latinx community, especially undocumented students. A graduate of LMU and the Graduate Theological Union Berkeley, she is a contributing writer for *America* magazine and publishes and speaks widely as a public theologian. Committed to a faith that does justice, she is an adviser to the Ignatian Solidarity Network, Catholic Women Preach, and the Discerning Deacons project. She is a respected international lecturer on issues of political theology, theological aesthetics, and Latino theology, and is the author of the book *Bridge to Wonder: Art as a Gospel of Beauty* (Baylor University Press, 2012), co-editor of *Teaching Global Theologies: Power and Praxis* (Baylor University Press, 2015), and a contributor to many other publications, including *Go into the Streets: The Welcoming Church of Pope Francis* and *Contemporary Art and Religion: A Curious Regard.*

Mary Ellen Green, OP
After graduating from Edgewood College in Madison, WI, with a French major, Mary Ellen entered the Dominican Sisters of Sinsinawa. She foolishly thought she would be teaching French to adolescents for the rest of her life. Was she mistaken! Mary Ellen has spent the last fifty years serving the People of God in many and varied ways. Her ministries have included preaching retreats in Ireland, France, Australia, and New Zealand as well as parish missions, adult faith formation, spiritual direction, financial development, congregation leadership, and five years as regional director of the Jesuit Volunteer Corps Southwest. At this time, Mary Ellen is living in retirement at Stair Crest in Muskego, WI, sharing life with her sisters and enjoying the opportunity to volunteer her services in many ways.

Margaret Eletta Guider, OSF
Margaret Eletta Guider, OSF, is associate professor of missiology at the Boston College School of Theology and Ministry and former department chair of the ecclesiastical faculty. Born and raised in Chicago, she completed undergraduate and graduate degrees in education at the University of Illinois Chicago. In 1975, she became a lay missioner and ministered in Goiás, Brazil, with the Sisters of St. Francis of Mary Im-

maculate. Upon her return to the United States, she entered the congregation, and she later returned to Chicago to serve as director of mission education for the archdiocese and as chaplain for the Cook County Juvenile Detention Center. Sr. Guider holds theological degrees from Catholic Theological Union, the Weston Jesuit School of Theology, and the Divinity School of Harvard University. Her most recent book is *The Grace of Medellín: History, Theology and Legacy: Reflections on the Significance of Medellín for the Church in the United States* (Convivium, 2018).

Kim R. Harris

Kim R. Harris is assistant professor of African American religious thought and practice in the Department of Theological Studies at Loyola Marymount University, Los Angeles. She holds a PhD in worship and the arts from Union Theological Seminary, New York City. Dr. Harris is a member of the Black Catholic Theological Symposium and the North American Academy of Liturgy. While pursuing her doctorate, she composed *Welcome Table: A Mass of Spirituals. Welcome Table* is a featured complete Mass setting in the second edition of the Black Catholic hymnal *Lead Me Guide Me* and the *Gather* hymnal 4th Edition (GIA Publications Inc.). Her current research concerns Black Catholic liturgy in a time of changing parish demographics and consolidations, as well as the need to diversify available liturgical resources for worship.

Andrea Hattler Bramson

A lifelong Catholic, Andrea Hattler Bramson is the second of the seven children of Denny and Carl Hattler. She spent many of her formative years living in Puerto Rico attending Sacred Heart schools and loving life in the tropics. She graduated from the University of South Carolina with a degree in art studio and retired from the federal government in September 2017 after thirty-plus years of service. Andrea has been the president of the Loyola Foundation for more than ten years, and has been a trustee for more than thirty. She has served on the boards of SOAR!, FADICA, ISN, and NCEA, and was the president of the pastoral council of her parish in Reston, Virginia. Andrea is the mother of three and lives in Bluffton, South Carolina, with Brian, her husband of more than thirty years, her daughters Addy and Victoria, and the two dogs that show anyone unconditional love.

Kristin Heyer

Kristin E. Heyer is professor of theological ethics at Boston College. She received her BA from Brown University and her PhD in theological ethics from Boston College. Her books include *Kinship across Borders: A Christian Ethic of Immigration* (Georgetown University Press, 2012) and *Prophetic and Public: The Social Witness of U.S. Catholicism* (Georgetown University Press, 2006). Prior to returning to Boston College, she taught at Loyola Marymount University and Santa Clara University. She teaches courses on moral agency, migration ethics, Catholic social thought, and HIV/AIDS. She serves as president of the Catholic Theological Society of America and co-chair of the planning committee for Catholic Theological Ethics in the World Church; she has served on the boards of the Moral Traditions Series at Georgetown University Press and the Seminar on Jesuit Higher Education. She and her husband, Mark Potter, are raising two sons in Newton, Massachusetts.

Mary Kate Holman

Mary Kate Holman is assistant professor of religious studies at Fairfield University. She earned her PhD in theology from

Fordham University in 2020 and taught for three years at Benedictine University near Chicago before returning to the East Coast. Her book on the French theologian Marie-Dominique Chenu is slated for publication by the University of Notre Dame Press in 2025, and her teaching and upcoming research focus on feminist theology and Ignatian spirituality.

Natalia Imperatori-Lee

Natalia Imperatori-Lee is professor of religious studies at Manhattan College in the Bronx, NY, where she also coordinates the Catholic Studies program. She is the author of *Cuéntame: Narrative in the Ecclesial Present* (Orbis Books, 2018). Her work focuses on the intersection of Latinx theologies, feminist theologies, and Catholic ecclesiology. A native of Miami, FL, she has served on the board of directors of the Catholic Theological Society of America and the Academy of Catholic Hispanic Theologians of the U.S. She recently presented at a series of seminars on the implementation of Pope Francis's *Amoris Laetitia*. At Manhattan College, Dr. Imperatori-Lee teaches courses on contemporary Catholicism, including Vatican II, as well as courses such as Sexuality and the Sacred and Women in Western Religion. She is currently working on a book about women in the Catholic Church. She lives in the Bronx.

Katie Lacz

Katie Lacz, MDiv, works as program director for the Women's Ordination Conference, the oldest and largest organization advocating for the ordination of women as deacons, priests, and bishops in an inclusive and accountable Roman Catholic Church. Katie has ministered to young people through Regis University's Catholic Campus Ministry Association's award-winning Romero House program, and as part of the staff of the Colorado Vincentian Volunteers. As a Jesuit Volunteer, she worked as a community organizer against the death penalty in North Carolina as part of People of Faith against the Death Penalty. Katie earned her MDiv from the Jesuit School of Theology of Santa Clara University in Berkeley, and her BA in journalism from Ithaca College. She is a spiritual director, a writer, and a contributor to the Ignatian Solidarity Network's *Rise Up* series. Born and raised in Schenectady, NY, she now lives outside Boulder, CO, with her husband, two children, and greyhound.

Valerie D. Lewis-Mosley
Dr. Valerie D. Lewis-Mosley is an alumna of Boston College School of Nursing, Seton Hall University School of Law, Seton Hall University School of Theology–Immaculate Conception Seminary, and Drew Theological School. Valerie has completed graduate studies in nursing leadership at New York University and is a graduate of Xavier University of Louisiana Institute for Black Catholic Studies. She also has doctrinal certification from the Archdiocese of Newark where she serves on the advisory board for the African-American African and Caribbean Apostolate. Valerie is an adjunct professor in the Department of Theology at Caldwell University and Xavier University of Louisiana Institute for Black Catholic Studies. She was the recipient of the Caldwell Dominican Peace Award for 2022, Aquinas Institute of Theology Delaplane Preaching Scholar of the 2022 Writing Cohort, and the Saint Katharine Drexel National Justice Award for 2023. Her writings include "Does Christian Catechesis Have a Gender Problem? Toward a Catechesis of Wholeness," in *Religion, Women of Color, and the Suffrage Movement: The Journey to Holistic Freedom* (Lexington Books, 2022), and "Preaching with an Unbridled Tongue," in *Preaching Racial Justice* (Orbis Books, 2023).

Kimberly Lymore

In 2000, Kimberly Lymore decided to leave corporate America and pursue full-time ministry. Kimberly has been a member of the Faith Community of St. Sabina since 1983 and was appointed full-time pastoral associate of the community by the Rev. Michael L. Pfleger on September 1, 2000. Kimberly is responsible for all the sacramental preparation of the children and adults. She is also the team leader for Eucharistic ministers. Kimberly is currently the convener of the Black Catholic Theological Symposium, as well as director of the Augustus Tolton Pastoral Ministry Program at Catholic Theological Union (CTU). Kimberly Lymore received her master of divinity degree with a concentration in Word from CTU, and she received her doctor of ministry from McCormick Theological Union. Her thesis was titled, "God Doesn't Tilt: Making the Connection between Worship and Justice."

Marie Anne Mayeski

With an advanced degree in English literature, Marie Anne taught in a Catholic high school for eight years. Seeking to be a better religion teacher, she took a course in New Testament theology that changed her intellectual and spiritual focus and the trajectory of her career. She received a PhD in theology from Fordham University and taught for more than thirty years in the Department of Theological Studies at Loyola Marymount University. Her areas of specialization were New Testament theology, early Christian history, and the place and accomplishments of women in Christian history. Her publications include *Women at the Table: Three Medieval Theologians* (Liturgical Press, 2004) and a childhood memoir entitled *Once upon a Different Time* (Upswing Publishing, 2019). Since 1987 she has served in various ministerial capacities in her Los Angeles parish, including preaching the homily at the Easter Vigil for almost twenty years.

Gina Messina

Gina Messina, PhD, serves as associate professor and executive director of the Institute for Women at Ursuline College where she formerly served as dean of the School of Graduate and Professional Studies. Prior to her time at Ursuline College, she served as the director of the Center for Women's Interdisciplinary Research and Education (WIRE) at Claremont Graduate University and as a visiting professor of theological ethics at Loyola Marymount University. She is the co-founder of Feminism and Religion and author of *Rape Culture and Spiritual Violence* (Routledge, 2014). She is also co-editor of *Faithfully Feminist: Jewish, Christian, and Muslim Feminists on Why We Stay* (with Jennifer Zobair and Amy Levin; White Cloud Press, 2015), *Feminism and Religion in the 21st Century* (with Rosemary Radford Ruether; Routledge, 2014), and *Women Religion Revolution* (with Xochitl Alvizo; Feminist Studies in Religion Books, 2017).

Jackie Minnock

Jackie Minnock was born in Dublin, Ireland. She contracted polio when she was a year old and is proud to be known as a polio survivor. Jackie now lives about an hour north of Dublin in County Louth. She has been married to Colm for more than thirty years and has two children and grandchildren. She completed her theology degree by distance education at the Priory Institute Dublin in 2011 and her master's degree in intercultural theology and interreligious studies at the School of Ecumenics at Trinity College Dublin in 2014. She has written for a number of theological journals and has broadcast on Irish National Radio's *Living Word*. She has also written a number of articles for *Polio Survivor* magazine in Ireland.

Jackie is a member of We Are Church Ireland and Root & Branch Lay Led Synod Group and is passionate about reform in the Catholic Church.

Catherine Mooney

Catherine Mooney teaches church history and the history of Christian spirituality at Boston College's School of Theology and Ministry. She has a master of theological studies (MTS) from Harvard Divinity School, and an MA, MPhil, and PhD in history from Yale University. She has served as president of the Hagiography Society and as board member for Monastic Matrix, a web resource about medieval women's religious communities; the Society for Medieval Feminist Studies; the Franciscan Friars; and the Jesuit-founded Bollandist Society. Catherine Mooney's publications include *Gendered Voices: Medieval Saints and Their Interpreters* (University of Pennsylvania Press, 1999), *Philippine Duchesne: A Woman with the Poor* (Wipf and Stock, 1990; 2007), *Clare of Assisi and the Thirteenth-Century Church: Religious Women, Rules, and Resistance* (University of Pennsylvania Press, 2016), which won the Hagiography Society's best book award in 2018; and *Filipina Duchesne: Una mujer con los pobres y marginados* (rev. ed., Kit, 2018).

Carmen Nanko-Fernández

A self-described Hurban@ (Hispanic and urban) theologian, Carmen is professor of Hispanic theology and ministry at Catholic Theological Union in Chicago. Her publications include the book *Theologizing en Espanglish* (Orbis Books, 2014) and numerous chapters and articles on Latin@ theologies, Catholic social teaching, im/migration, and sport and theology. She is currently completing *¿El Santo? Baseball and the Canonization of Roberto Clemente*, which is under contract for the Sport and Religion series of Mercer University Press.

Carmen has presented in a variety of academic and pastoral venues, including a conference at the National Baseball Hall of Fame in Cooperstown, NY. A past president of the Academy of Catholic Hispanic Theologians of the United States (ACHTUS), she received its Virgilio Elizondo Award for "distinguished achievement in theology." Carmen's writings have appeared in *Commonweal* and the *National Catholic Reporter*. She is the founding co-editor of the multivolume series Disruptive Cartographers: Doing Theology Latinamente (Fordham University Press).

Mary J. Novak

Mary J. Novak serves as executive director of NETWORK Lobby for Catholic Social Justice in Washington, DC. Previously, Mary served Georgetown University Law Center as a mission integrator and adjunct professor of law. Mary practiced law for more than a decade in the areas of California water, energy, and environmental and natural resources while also serving on a team pursuing a capital appeal for a man on the largest death row in the United States. She later joined Santa Clara University, first as a member of the clinical law faculty and later as the director for faculty development in what is now the Ignatian Center for Jesuit Education. Mary is a peacebuilding practitioner, having studied at Eastern Mennonite University's Center for Justice and Peacebuilding. She is an Associate of the Congregation of St. Joseph (CSJ) and the founding board chair of the Catholic Mobilizing Network to end the use of the death penalty and promote restorative justice.

Anne Celestine Ondigo, FSJ

Sr. Anne Celestine Ondigo is a member of the Franciscan Sisters of St. Joseph–Kenya currently residing in Perry, NY. She is a former lecturer at the Centre for Social Justice and Ethics at the Catholic University of Eastern Africa and in the Department of Peace and International Relations at Daystar University. She has worked with Franciscans International in Geneva, advocating for human rights and peace for African countries by networking with human rights activists at the grassroots level to air their needs at the Universal Periodic Review at the United Nations office. She has also worked with the Justice, Peace and Integrity of Creation Africa Office as the organizing secretary. She is a proud member of Catholic Theological Ethics in the World Church. Sr. Anne Celestine is a postdoctoral researcher at Boston College, and holds a PhD in diplomacy, peace, and international relations.

Carolyn Osiek, RSCJ

Carolyn Osiek, RSCJ, was professor of New Testament at Catholic Theological Union at Chicago for twenty-six years, and is professor emerita at Brite Divinity School at Texas Christian University. She retired in 2009 to become provincial archivist of the Society of the Sacred Heart, United States–Canada Province. She is the author or editor of many books and articles on the topics of the New Testament and the early church, and of the early history of the Society of the Sacred Heart.

Yvonne Prowse

Yvonne Prowse, MA, is a spiritual director and trainer and supervisor of spiritual directors. She has been leading retreats and lecturing on spirituality for more than three decades, with emphasis on eco-spirituality and feminine spirituality. She teaches many aspects of spiritual direction and Ignatian spirituality and served for over a decade as the chair/co-chair of spiritual direction training at Loyola House in Guelph, Ontario,

Canada. Yvonne holds an MA in spirituality and spiritual direction from Fordham University. She has also trained with indigenous elders of North America and Burkina Faso. Her earlier ministries in the U.S. included care for homeless adults and children and interfaith peace and justice work. She is co-author of an upcoming book for parishes on ecological conversion; author of "Spiritual Direction and the Call to Ecological Conversion" in *Presence* (December 2016); and was leader of the contemplative retreat for the annual conference of Spiritual Directors International (SDI) in 2017.

Barbara Quinn, RSCJ

Barbara Quinn, RSCJ, is a member of the Society of the Sacred Heart, United States–Canada Province. Since 2011, she has been serving as the associate director of spiritual formation at the Boston College School of Theology and Ministry. Prior to that, Barbara served for ten years as the founding director of the Center for Christian Spirituality at the University of San Diego. She holds a bachelor of arts degree in psychology from Rosemont College, a master of divinity from the Weston Jesuit School of Theology, and a doctor of ministry from the Catholic Theological Union. Barbara was the founder of Leadership Development for Ministry in Buffalo, NY, a formation program to train laity from various Christian denominations for leadership in their churches. She continued to develop and administer a similar program in Anchorage, AK. Barbara has facilitated retreats and days of renewal in the U.S., Uganda, France, Ireland, Australia, Japan, and India.

Emily Rauer Davis

Emily Rauer Davis is associate director of the Office of the College Chaplains at the College of the Holy Cross in

Worcester, MA. A 1999 graduate of Holy Cross, she spent a year with the Jesuit Volunteer Corps in Fresno, CA, before receiving her master of divinity degree at Weston Jesuit School of Theology. Her previous work in ministry has involved both high school and college campus ministry, young adult spirituality programming, and faculty/staff formation. She has spent most of her career at Jesuit institutions, including Loyola University Maryland, Seattle University, and the Ignatian Spirituality Center in Seattle. Emily has also written for the Ignatian Solidarity Network's *Just Parenting* blog. A native of Syracuse, NY, Emily currently lives in Natick, MA, with her husband, Andrew, and their two sons, Michael and Peter.

Verónica Rayas

Verónica Rayas, PhD, is director of the Office of Religious Education in the Diocese of El Paso. She holds a PhD in religious education from Fordham University. Her doctoral thesis, titled "The Family's Catechesis: The Mexican American Family as a Place of Catechesis through Their Spirituality," focused on the catechetical principles present in the traditions and life of faith of many Mexican American families. Verónica has had extensive experience in various ministries, including catechist, youth ministry, Catholic school teacher, and pastoral associate.

Jane E. Regan

Dr. Jane E. Regan is associate professor emerita of theology at the School of Theology and Ministry at Boston College and former director of Continuing Education for the School of Theology and Ministry. Her academic background, which includes a PhD in religious education from the Catholic University of America, is complemented by her educational and pastoral work. She has been involved in religious education at the diocesan and national levels for many years. Dr. Regan is a nationally recognized speaker whose particular focus is on adult faith formation and catechetical leadership.

Joan Rosenhauer

Joan Rosenhauer is president of Jesuit Refugee Service/USA. As a member of JRS's global senior leadership team, she also helps lead JRS's global operations. She is a former JRS/USA board member and has spent most of her career advocating for social justice and mobilizing the U.S. Catholic community to do the same. As the executive vice president of Catholic Relief Services, she led the organization's outreach, advocacy, marketing, and communications. Prior to joining CRS, she spent sixteen years with the U.S. Conference of Catholic Bishops, where she served as associate director of the Department of Justice, Peace, and Human Development. She has a bachelor's degree in social work from the University of Iowa and a master's degree in public policy management from the University of Maryland, and she has been awarded honorary doctorates from Dominican College, St. Ambrose University, and Georgetown University.

Grace Salceanu

Grace Salceanu is an educator and campus minister in the Bay Area. Her work has included co-directing global education programs in the Philippines and El Salvador, leading retreats, organizing spiritual formation for youth and adults in San Francisco, and teaching theology. She is a director of the Spiritual Exercises of St. Ignatius. Her other callings include being a mother to a vibrant seven-year-old and partner to her husband. Spiritual lessons abound in both her professional and family life. She is grateful for all the resilient, tenacious, and dynamic people and communities who have formed, inspired, challenged, and illuminated how God is at work in everything.

Carmen Sammut, MSOLA

Carmen Sammut, MSOLA, was born and lived her first twenty-two years on the island of Malta. She was trained as a teacher and taught for three years before joining the Missionary Sisters of Our Lady of Africa (MSOLA) in 1974. She completed her religious studies and training in London, England, and Ottawa, Canada. She obtained a degree in Rome in Arabic and Islamic studies. Apart from two years in Malawi, her missionary experience has involved interreligious dialogue in Muslim countries. She lived for fifteen years in Tunisia, nine years in Algeria, and three years in Mauritania before becoming, from 2011 to 2023, congregational leader based in Rome. She was president of the International Union of Superiors General (UISG) from 2013 to 2019.

Flora X. Tang

Flora X. Tang is a doctoral candidate in theology and peace studies at the University of Notre Dame, where she writes and does research on post-traumatic theology, queer theology, and literature from the Asian diaspora. She received her master's in theological studies from Harvard Divinity School. Flora has previously worked as a hospital chaplain, a campus ministry fellow, and a service-learning program coordinator for college students. Her theology and preaching draw from her complex faith journey to and within Catholicism: from becoming Catholic at age nineteen after living and serving with Catholic sisters, to deconstructing her faith while living in Palestine, to discovering her own queer Catholic expressions of faith. Flora is committed to reimagining God's love while standing on the margins of the Catholic faith. Flora's writings appear in the *National Catholic Reporter* and *America* magazine, and her book of poetry has been published in Mandarin Chinese. She is originally from Beijing, China, and currently lives in South Bend, IN, with her occasional foster cats and kittens.

Sia Nyasari Temu

Sia Nyasari Temu is a Maryknoll Sister from Tanzania. A trained secondary school teacher, she taught mathematics and physics before joining the Maryknoll Sisters. Presently she is working in Kenya. A Maryknoll Sister for twenty years, Sia has been privileged to intentionally live in an intercultural community for more than ten years. She has facilitated intercultural living workshops in both male and female religious houses in Kenya. She is a facilitator of conversations for social change programs in different parts of Kenya that have been experiencing conflict. In addition, Sia facilitates Engaging Our Complexities among Maryknoll Sisters. Sia holds a bachelor of theology from Catholic University of Eastern Africa, a graduate certificate in pastoral studies from Catholic Theological Union, and a certificate in trauma awareness and transformation from the Summer Peacebuilding Institute of the Center for Justice and Peacebuilding at Eastern Mennonite University. She loves nature, gardening, and creating safe space for multi-perspective conversations.

Jennifer Theby-Quinn

Jennifer Theby-Quinn is a professional actor, vocalist, educator, and campus minister. She currently serves as a campus minister focusing on the Graduate Student/Young Adult Community and Women's Community at the Catholic Student Center at Washington University in St. Louis. Jen also heads Upper Room, an undergraduate spiritual and theological formation program she had a hand in creating. Jen completed her undergraduate education in theology and theatre performance at Saint Louis University and spent eight months as a mainstage and touring actor for the Shakespeare Festival–Saint Louis, before following the Holy Spirit to a position as director of campus ministry at Visitation Academy, an all-girls prep school. She also taught middle school theology at the Academy of the Sacred Heart. Jen has a master's degree in theology and a certificate in biblical study (New Testament) from Aquinas Institute of Theology. Jen lives with her beloved husband, son, and two snuggly pups.

Elizabeth Turnwald
Elizabeth Turnwald is the assistant director for tutor engagement and tutor chaplain with EVkids in Boston. Originally from northwestern Ohio, she holds an MDiv from the Boston College School of Theology and Ministry and a BA in music and Spanish with a minor in women's and gender studies from the University of Dayton. She previously served as a Jesuit Volunteer in New York City, where she was the retreat coordinator and conflict resolution program assistant at the Tanenbaum Center for Interreligious Understanding. She is a board member for Sacred Threads, a Boston-based, non-denominational, non-profit organization committed to nourishing, connecting and inspiring women by weaving spirituality into everyday life. She is currently in training to become a certified Enneagram teacher through the Narrative Enneagram.

Yadira Vieyra Alvarez
Yadira Vieyra Alvarez is a developmental/infant mental health specialist at Erikson Institute. For five years, she worked at the School of Social Service Administration at the University of

Chicago doing research in the field of early childhood intervention. Yadira has also collaborated with the University of Illinois Chicago and Immaculate Conception Parish in Brighton Park through "Fortaleciendo mi familia"—a series of sessions aimed at providing low-intensity cognitive behavioral therapy and psychosocial support to Mexican immigrant families. She attended Cristo Rey Jesuit High School in Chicago and completed her bachelor's degree in psychology and theology at Georgetown University. She received her master of science degree from Erikson Institute in Chicago. In 2018, she served as an auditor at the Synod of Bishops on Young People, the Faith, and Vocational Discernment, representing the immigrant community in the United States.

Wamũyũ Teresia Wachira, IBVM

Wamũyũ Teresia Wachira is a Kenyan and member of the Institute of the Blessed Virgin Mary (IBVM). She earned her PhD in peace studies from the University of Bradford, United Kingdom; a master's degree in applied theology, peace, and justice studies, from Middlesex University, United Kingdom; and a bachelor's degree in education from Kenyatta University, Nairobi, Kenya. She has been a teacher and principal in Loreto schools in Kenya, specializing in training young women for peacemaking and reconciliation work. She is a senior lecturer and program leader of the Peace and Conflict studies at St. Paul University in Nairobi, Kenya. She is co-president, Pax Christi International, and a member of the Pan-African Catholic Theology and Pastoral Network. In addition to training and advocating for termination of female genital mutilation, she is an ardent, committed peace scholar and peacebuilder and advocates for active nonviolence as a spirituality, way of life, and effective method of preventing and addressing violence.

Sister Jane Wakahiu, LSOSF, PhD

Sister Jane Wakahiu, LSOSF, PhD, is a member of the institute of the Little Sisters of Saint Francis, Kenya. She provides leadership to and direction of the Conrad N. Hilton Foundation's Program Department and oversees planning, development, implementation, and evaluation of the Catholic Sisters Initiative. Prior to joining the foundation, she was the executive director of the African Sisters Education Collaborative (ASEC). She has taught extensively at the undergraduate and graduate levels and has broad educational and administrative experience gained from serving as a teacher and administrator at a high school in Kenya and leading women's organizations. She authored *Transformative Partnerships: The Role of Agencies, Church and Religious Institutes in Promoting Strategic Social and Sustainable Change in Africa.* She holds a PhD in human development and higher education administration from Marywood University, an MA from Saint Bonaventure University, and a bachelor of education from the Catholic University of Eastern Africa.

Julia Walsh

Sister Julia Walsh is a Franciscan Sister of Perpetual Adoration and part of her congregation's formation team, serving women who are discerning their vocation. Along with another Franciscan Sister, she co-founded The Fireplace, an intentional community and house of hospitality on Chicago's South Side that offers spiritual support to seekers, artists, and activists. She has a MA in pastoral studies from Catholic Theological Union and is a spiritual director and secondary school teacher. As a creative writer, educator, retreat presenter, and speaker she is passionate about exploring the intersection of creativity, spirituality, activism, and community life. A regularly published spiritual writer, Sister Julia's work can be found in publications such as *America, Living Faith Catholic Devotional, National Catholic Reporter, Chicago Sun Times, Living City,* and *St. Anthony Messenger.* She hosts the *Messy Jesus Business* blog and podcast. She is the author of the spiritual memoir *For Love of the Broken Body* (Monkfish, 2024).

Kerry Weber

Kerry Weber is an executive editor for *America* magazine, where she has worked since 2009. Her writing and multimedia work have earned several awards from the Catholic Media Association, including Writer of the Year in 2023. Kerry is the author of *Mercy in the City: How to Feed the Hungry, Give Drink to the Thirsty, Visit the Imprisoned, and Keep Your Day Job* (Loyola Press, 2014). A graduate of Providence College and Columbia University Graduate School of Journalism, she is a board member of the Catholic Media Association and has been a Mercy Associate since 2012. Her work has appeared in the *Washington Post, The Atlantic,* and *Sojourners.* She lives in western Massachusetts with her husband and three children.

Jenny Wiertel

Jenny Wiertel holds an MDiv from the University of Notre Dame and a BS from Georgetown University. She has served in campus ministry, residential life, hospital chaplaincy, and Catholic Worker spaces. She currently lives and works in Phoenix, AZ, at Andre House of Hospitality, a ministry inspired by Holy Cross spirituality and the Catholic Worker movement. Jenny is passionate about amplifying the voices of those who are marginalized in our Church and in our world.

Deborah Wilhelm

Deborah Wilhelm, DMin, is adjunct professor of preaching and evangelization at the Aquinas Institute of Theology, where she co-directs the Delaplane Preaching Initiative. In addition, she lectures in practical theology at Loyola University New Orleans. She is co-author and co-editor with Gregory Heille and Maurice Nutt of *Preaching Racial Justice* (Orbis Books, 2023); co-author with Bishop Sylvester Ryan of *Preaching Matters: A Praxis for Preachers* (Paul Bechtold Library Publications, 2015); and co-author of the 2023 Year A and 2024 Year B editions of *Living the Word* (GIA Publications). Deborah has also written numerous chapters and articles for scholarly, professional, and general-audience publications. She preaches at the Dominican site theWord, and she speaks and leads retreats as time permits. As a Camaldolese Benedictine oblate, Deborah strives to live as a beginner in all things and to receive those who cross her path as Christ. Deborah and her husband live in the rural Western United States.